COPING WITH A
NUCLEARIZING IRAN

JAMES DOBBINS, ALIREZA NADER,
DALIA DASSA KAYE, FREDERIC WEHREY

NATIONAL SECURITY
RESEARCH DIVISION

The research described in this report was sponsored by the Smith Richardson Foundation.

Library of Congress Control Number: 2011942595

ISBN: 978-0-8330-5865-2

The RAND Corporation is a nonprofit institution that helps improve policy and decisionmaking through research and analysis. RAND's publications do not necessarily reflect the opinions of its research clients and sponsors.

RAND® is a registered trademark.

Cover photos (clockwise from top left): Iran's supreme leader Ayatollah Ali Khamenei (AP/Hasan Sarbakhshian); President Barack Obama (AP/Carolyn Kaster); Revolutionary Guard's Tondar missile is launched in a drill (AP/Fars News Agency, Ali Shaigan); Iranian President Mahmoud Ahmadinejad (AP/Hasan Sarbakhshian).

Published 2011 by the RAND Corporation
1776 Main Street, P.O. Box 2138, Santa Monica, CA 90407-2138
1200 South Hayes Street, Arlington, VA 22202-5050
4570 Fifth Avenue, Suite 600, Pittsburgh, PA 15213-2665
RAND URL: http://www.rand.org/
To order RAND documents or to obtain additional information, contact
Distribution Services: Telephone: (310) 451-7002;
Fax: (310) 451-6915; Email: order@rand.org

Preface

The research described in this report was sponsored by the Smith Richardson Foundation and conducted within the International Security and Defense Policy Center of the RAND National Security Research Division (NSRD). NSRD conducts research and analysis on defense and national security topics for the U.S. and allied defense, foreign policy, homeland security, and intelligence communities and foundations and other nongovernmental organizations that support defense and national security analysis.

For more information on the International Security and Defense Policy Center, see http://www.rand.org/nsrd/about/isdp.html or contact the director (contact information is provided on web page).

Contents

Preface iii
Summary ix
Acknowledgments xxiii
Abbreviations xxv

CHAPTER ONE
Introduction 1

CHAPTER TWO
U.S. Interests, Objectives, and Strategies 3
Long History of Mutual Grievances 4
Ups and Downs in the Relationship 6

CHAPTER THREE
Iran's Interests, Objectives, and Strategies 9
Iranian Views of the United States 11
Iranian Factional Interests 12
Ideological Opposition to the United States 16
The Revolutionary Guards 20
Iran's Future Nuclear Posture 24
Conclusion 27

CHAPTER FOUR
The Other Actors 29
The Gulf Cooperation Council States 30
Key Areas of U.S. Leverage 39

Israel 42
  Halting Iran's Nuclear Capabilities 42
  Constraining Iran's Regional Influence 44
  Influencing Iran's Internal Political Evolution 44
Turkey 50
Syria 56
Iraq 59
China 61
Russia 63
Europe 66
Conclusion 68

CHAPTER FIVE
U.S. Instruments and Iranian Vulnerabilities 71
Diplomacy 71
  Third-Party Intermediaries 72
  Multilateral Diplomacy 74
  Direct U.S.-Iranian Dialogue 75
  Iran's Political System and U.S. Diplomacy 78
Sanctions 79
Covert Action 84
Soft Power 86
The Military Option 89
  Halting Iran's Nuclear Program 90
  Moderating Iranian External Behavior 90
Influencing Iran's Internal Evolution 91
Conclusion 91

CHAPTER SIX
Policy Alternatives 93
Engagement 94
Containment 95
Preemption 96
Deterrence 97
Normalization 98

Regime Change 99
Conclusion 99

CHAPTER SEVEN
Coping with a Nuclearizing Iran 101
Containment Plus.. 103
  Deterrence 104
  Sanctions... 106
  Engagement.. 107
  Soft Power 108

Bibliography 111

Summary

It is not inevitable that Iran will acquire nuclear weapons or that it will gain the capacity to quickly produce them. American and even Israeli analysts continually push their estimates for such an event further into the future. Nevertheless, absent a change in Iranian policy, it is reasonable to assume that, some time in the coming decade, Iran will acquire such a capability. Western policymakers shy away from addressing this prospect, lest they seem to be acquiescing to something they deem unacceptable and want to prevent. But there is a big difference between acknowledging and accepting another's behavior. It is unacceptable that Iran should even be seeking nuclear weapons in violation of its treaty commitments, yet the U.S. government nevertheless acknowledges that Iran is doing so because that admission is a necessary prerequisite to effectively addressing the problem.

Most recent scholarly studies have also focused on how to prevent Iran from acquiring nuclear weapons. Other, less voluminous writing looks at what to do after Iran becomes a nuclear power. What has so far been lacking is a policy framework for dealing with Iran before, after, and, indeed, during its crossing of the nuclear threshold. Herein, we try to fill that gap by providing a midterm strategy for dealing with Iran that neither begins nor ends at the point at which Tehran acquires a nuclear weapon capability. We propose an approach that neither acquiesces to a nuclear-armed Iran nor refuses to admit the possibility—indeed, the likelihood—of this occurring.

U.S. Objectives

The United States has three main objectives with respect to Iran: restraining its external behavior, moderating its domestic politics, and reversing its nuclear weapon program. U.S. policy should be designed to advance all three goals. Progress toward any one objective would probably help advance the others, or at least make their achievement less urgent. Yet there are also tensions between the three objectives, or at least between the policies intended to advance them. Containment isolates Iranian reformists, as well as the repressive elements of Iranian society. Sanctions help rally public opinion around the regime and increase popular support for its nuclear ambitions. U.S. efforts to promote political reform are used by the regime both to justify repression and to discredit the opposition.

Since the 1979 Iranian revolution, containment of Iranian external influence has been the dominant U.S. objective regarding Iran, accompanied by occasional efforts at engagement and limited bouts of armed conflict. Isolating Iran was relatively easy as long as the country faced hostile adversaries to both east and west. It was Iraqi misbehavior, not Iranian, that first brought U.S. ground and air forces into the Persian Gulf in 1990 and has kept them there ever since. The U.S. invasions of Afghanistan and Iraq replaced regimes hostile to both Iran and the United States with ones friendly to both. With these two adversaries eliminated, Iran and the United States began to identify each other as the dominant challenge.

Iranian Objectives

Iran and the United States both have substantial reasons for their mutual antipathy. Iranian grievances go back to the U.S. role in overthrowing Iran's democratically elected government in 1953, followed by Washington's backing of the shah for the next 26 years, and then U.S. support for Saddam Hussein's war of aggression against Iran, during which the U.S. Navy shot down an Iranian civil airliner over international waters in the Persian Gulf. U.S. grievances began with the seizure of the U.S. embassy and the holding hostage of its staff in 1979, followed by Iranian links to terrorist attacks on U.S. forces in Beirut in 1983 and in Saudi Arabia in 1996 and Iranian support for extremist movements in Lebanon, Gaza, Iraq, and Afghanistan. In the past decade, however, Iran's nuclear program has emerged as the dominant U.S. concern. Most recently, Iran's alleged involvement in terrorist attacks on Saudi and Israeli targets in the United States adds yet a new source of conflict.

The anti-American and anti-Israeli elements of Iranian policy have historical and ideological roots, but they are also geopolitically instrumental, offering the regime a means of going over the heads of hostile Arab governments to directly influence their populations. Iran has no modern history of military aggression and only limited capabilities to threaten its neighbors militarily. It is not, however, the Iranian military that its neighbors fear most, but rather the Islamic Republic's appeal to its neighbors' populations as the ideological bastion of anti-American, anti-Israeli, and pro-Shi'a sentiment; as the patron of Arab rejectionist forces; and as a source of funding, advice, and arms for insurgent and extremist groups

Iran's odd combination of theocracy and elected institutions has produced generally cautious and pragmatic behavior at the state-to-state level, combined with the use of subversion, terrorism, propaganda, ideology, and religion to undermine neighboring regimes it regards as adversaries. Conservative and reformist governments have sometimes sought to emphasize the overt and more positive strain of Iranian policy, but the security establishment and the religious leadership have never been willing to entirely abandon the darker tools of statecraft. Iran continues to sponsor and train terrorist and insurgent groups throughout the Middle East. Controversy in Iran over the results of the 2009 Iranian presidential election have strengthened this latter, more fundamentalist faction, consolidating the power of the Revolutionary Guards and the position of the Supreme Leader, Ayatollah Ali Khamenei, as the final arbiter of Iranian policy. As long as these forces remain dominant, there is little prospect of overcoming the many differences that divide the United States and Iran, least of all that of Iran's nuclear program.

International Reactions

Arab regimes, particularly the smaller Persian Gulf monarchies, have responded to Iranian behavior with a mixture of fear and caution, looking to the Untied States for protection while keeping open lines of communication with Tehran and often avoiding too open an alignment with Washington, most notably on the Iranian nuclear program.

Europe, for its part, was reluctant to embrace George W. Bush's early emphasis on preemption as a response to nuclear proliferation. As Bush in his second term and then Barack Obama tempered this bellicose rhetoric, the major European powers began to align themselves more closely with Washington's efforts to employ mounting sanctions to stem the Iranian nuclear program. Russia and China have done likewise, albeit more cautiously.

Regional states and global powers are currently fairly united in opposing the Iranian nuclear program, but few do so with the concentration that marks U.S. policy. For most other governments, Israel aside, its nuclear program is one consideration regarding Iran among many. The Obama administration has, nevertheless, been quite successful in securing broad international support for sanctions on Iran. Most major European countries and U.S. allies have acceded to international sanctions against Iran and have curtailed business ties with the Islamic Republic. This coalition remains fragile, however, and probably cannot be led too much further absent some new Iranian provocation.

Regional governments are more worried about Iranian subversion than Iranian invasion. Most are equally as antipathetic to U.S. aspirations for their political evolution as they are to Iranian, rejecting as they do both models of governance. The Arab monarchies of the Gulf will likely resist the domestic reforms that offer the best antidote to Iranian influence, and they will offer little support for U.S. efforts to encourage Iranian democracy.

The Iranian leadership professes to believe that the Arab Spring will ultimately redound to Iran's benefit. Other observers feel that it is the United States that will gain influence as the result of democratization in the region. Perhaps the more likely result is a loss of influence for both Iran and the United States.

Iran has nothing to offer the democratizing Arab societies, either as a model or a source of assistance. Tehran's main source of leverage in the Arab world has been its capacity to undermine the legitimacy of authoritarian regimes linked to Washington and, by association, to Israel. Popularly based Arab regimes will reduce those links and therefore be less vulnerable to that kind of criticism. They will be less dependent on the United States, less friendly to Israel, and consequently less vulnerable to Iranian propaganda. They might become less hostile to Tehran but will also be less concerned about its ability to appeal directly to their publics.

The Gulf monarchies regard the Arab Spring as a threat to their own stability. This will increase their fear of the ideological challenge posed not just by Iran but also by democratizing Arab states and U.S. support for that process. These regimes will thus become more wary in their relations with both Tehran and Washington.

Syria might be an exception to this pattern of regional distancing both from Tehran and Washington. A more popularly based regime in Damascus would probably loosen its ties to Tehran while strengthening relations with the United States. This might prove a real regional game changer.

U.S. Instruments of Influence

The United States will be able to exert only a modest level of influence on Iran in the short and medium terms. U.S. diplomatic leverage is constrained by the bitter history of U.S.-Iranian relations and the domestic legitimacy the regime derives from defying the United States. The 2009 Iranian presidential election and the resulting divisions among political elites and within Iranian society at large have made the Islamic Republic even less susceptible to direct U.S. diplomatic influence, although these events also make Iran more vulnerable to U.S. economic leverage and soft power. The regime's conservative and principlist decisionmakers, ascendant in the postelection period, are unlikely to be swayed by U.S. efforts at engagement. Their repression and extremism, on the other hand, make it easier for the United

States to rally international pressure against them, while their domestic opposition is clearly looking outside Iran for inspiration, if not material support.

U.S. and international sanctions against Iran, particularly United Nations (UN) resolution 1929 (2010) and the Comprehensive Iran Sanctions, Accountability, and Divestment Act (CISADA) (Pub. L. 111-195, 2010), have significantly undermined Iran's economy and widened divisions within the regime. Even if these sanctions have little effect on Iranian policy, they very substantially degrade Iranian economic and military capability and thus limit the regime's capacity to project power and influence—a long-standing objective of U.S. policy.

Intelligence operations offer an opportunity to pay back the Iranian regime in its own coin. The Stuxnet computer virus attack on Natanz and the assassination of Iranian nuclear scientists, which some have attributed to Israeli intelligence agencies,[1] might have slowed the nuclear program and possibly helped bring Iran to the negotiation table in 2010–2011. However, such covert actions are used by the Iranian regime to justify more repression, and they probably also intensify its resolve to continue with the nuclear program.

The Iranian populace is more susceptible to U.S. influences on cultural and social matters than to Washington's views on foreign and security policy. Iran's drive in becoming economically, technologically, and militarily self-sufficient hinders U.S. economic and diplomatic leverage on the nuclear program. As a revolutionary state, the Islamic Republic is willing to absorb a significant amount of pain and isolation in order to achieve "independence," regional power, and prestige. However, the regime will not be able to stifle indefinitely popular demands for a more democratic, accountable, and open political system. Consistent U.S. support for these values, espoused across the region and not just targeted at Iran, offers the best hope of eventually achieving all three of the United States's prime objectives.

---

[1]   Broad, Markoff, and Sanger, 2011.

Policy Alternatives

Competing U.S. approaches toward Iran might be characterized as engagement versus containment, preemption versus deterrence, and normalization versus regime change. In effect, these are competing archetypes, offering three policy spectrums from which actual courses of action can be chosen. Since much of the policy debate in the United States turns around these archetypes, it is useful to examine how each might meet basic U.S. objectives before turning to a possible synthesis.

A policy of pure engagement would emphasize the use of diplomacy to resolve differences while seeking to increase travel, cultural exchanges, and commerce between the United States and Iran. Such a policy is unlikely to advance U.S. objectives as long as the principlists and Revolutionary Guards remain ascendant in Tehran.

By contrast, a policy of pure containment would employ defensive alliances, sanctions, and noncommunication to isolate and penalize Iran. Such an approach can achieve the objective of restraining Iran's external behavior, but it works against the goal of reforming its domestic politics, and it increases popular, as well as regime, support for the acquisition of nuclear weapons.

Preemption goes beyond mere containment to include an offensive threat or use of military force to forestall some unwanted development—in Iran's case, the acquisition of a nuclear weapon capability. Such an approach could slow Iran's nuclear program, but it would strengthen both external sympathy and internal support for the regime, as well as probably accelerating its efforts to acquire nuclear weapons. Containing Iran's regional influence would therefore become more difficult in the aftermath of a military strike.

Deterrence, by contrast, would employ the threat of retaliation to dissuade Iran from employing nuclear weapons to influence, coerce, or damage others. Such a policy is a necessary companion to containment should Iran cross the nuclear threshold. If deterrence is not accompanied by a greater level of engagement, however, the risk of uncontrolled escalation is high.

Normalization would involve mutual diplomatic recognition, exchange of ambassadors, and the opening of embassies. Given that

Iran already has diplomats stationed in both New York and Washington, it is the United States that would have the most to gain from the resumption of diplomatic relations. For this reason, among others, there is no prospect of such a development anytime soon.

Pure regime change, on the other hand, would involve the use of overt and covert efforts to delegitimize and destabilize the Iranian regime. Although the goal might be eminently desirable, most of the possible methods to achieve it would be likely to yield the opposite effect, perpetuating the current regime and strengthening its more-extreme elements.

Thus, none of these approaches, taken in isolation, offers the prospect of advancing all three of the United States's main objectives. Pure engagement will get nowhere with the current Iranian regime. Containment constrains only Iran's external behavior. Preemption deals only with the nuclear issue, and then only temporarily, while making progress toward the other two objectives more difficult. Deterrence is an appropriate complement to containment but, again, affects only Iran's external behavior. Neither normalization nor regime change is an attainable short-term objective.

Coping with a Nuclearizing Iran

Theoretically, the spectrum of possible Iranian nuclear capability runs from no program, civil or military, at one end, to a growing arsenal of tested weapons and long-range delivery systems at the other. Although the United States and much of the rest of the world would like to confine the Iranian program to the lowest possible level, there is strong support within Iran, across the political spectrum, within and without the government, for full mastery of the nuclear fuel cycle and, possibly, growing support within the populace for acquiring nuclear weapons.

The closer Iran moves toward testing and deploying nuclear weapons, the more negative the consequences for regional and global security. Uncertainty regarding Iran's actual capacity—although itself a source of anxiety—would be less provocative than certainty about such a capacity. The region has lived with an unacknowledged Israeli nuclear arsenal since the late 1960s and could conceivably do the same with a similarly discreet Iranian capacity. Better yet would be a certainty, derived from intrusive verification measures, that Iran, although capable of manufacturing nuclear weapons, had not actually done so. Worst of all would be a situation in which Iran had openly breached the Treaty on the Non-Proliferation of Nuclear Weapons (also known as the Non-Proliferation Treaty, or NPT), tested and deployed nuclear weapons, and begun to articulate a doctrine for their use. This latter situation would be the most likely to prompt other states to go down this same path while maximizing the levels of tension and anxiety among regional governments and populations.

Current U.S. policy is to offer an easing of sanctions only if Iran agrees to roll back its nuclear program by abandoning enrichment. There is no support for such a step anywhere on the Iranian political spectrum and, therefore, little prospect that this objective can be attained. We therefore recommend that the United States move toward a set of graduated objectives, seeking in the short term to dissuade Iran from actually testing and deploying nuclear weapons, while retaining the leverage necessary to eventually secure full Iranian compliance with its NPT obligations.

Iran is seeking nuclear weapons for some combination of security, influence, and prestige. Persuading the Iranian leadership that renouncing the NPT and building, testing, and deploying nuclear weapons will increase its isolation, diminish its influence, and confirm its pariah status is the best way of dissuading the regime from crossing that threshold. This effort at persuasion cannot really begin until the United States acknowledges that the Iranian program probably will not be reversed and thus commences preparations to deal with the consequences.

An all-or-nothing U.S. approach, one that insists on full rollback of enrichment before any easing of sanctions can take place, risks allowing the best to become the enemy of the good because neither the current nor any future regime in Iran is likely to agree to accept restrictions over and above those required by the NPT. On the other hand, a full abandonment of sanctions in exchange for a promise not to weaponize, even if fully monitored, would still leave Iran out of compliance with its other treaty obligations. Sanctions should, therefore, be deployed for both long- and short-term purposes. The long-term objective should be to bring Iran fully into compliance with the NPT. The short-term objective should be to halt the Iranian program short of weaponization.

Containment Plus

Containment will remain at the core of U.S. policy as long as Iran continues to subvert and threaten its neighbors. This will be true whether or not Iran possesses a nuclear arsenal but will be harder to achieve if it does. Harder still would be containing the regional influence of an Iran that had been the target of an unprovoked U.S. or Israeli attack.

Containment of a nuclear-armed Iran will need to be complemented by deterrence, to counterbalance the threat of nuclear use or blackmail; by sanctions, to offer the eventual hope of rolling back that capability; by engagement, to manage such confrontations that might occur; and by the employment of soft power, in order to advance the day when containment will cease to be necessary. Only such a combination of policies offers the possibility of advancing all three main U.S. objectives.

Deterrence

The United States successfully deterred a much more powerful Soviet Union for more than 40 years. Some argue that Iran is different, that its leaders are irrational, and that the threat of devastating retaliation would not dissuade it from employing or threatening to employ nuclear weapons. Although this fear is understandable, given occasionally heated Iranian rhetoric, there is nothing in the Islamic Republic's actual behavior throughout its existence to substantiate the charge of irrationality, let alone suicidal lunacy. Khamenei and President Mahmoud Ahmadinejad, whatever their other flaws, are models of mental health and restrained behavior compared with Joseph Stalin or Mao Zedong.

A more reasonable apprehension is not that nuclear deterrence would not work but rather that it would. A nuclear-armed Iran would be able to deter the United States from reacting forcefully to Iranian misbehavior. With the threat of U.S. (and Israeli) retaliation effectively removed, Iran could employ its nonmilitary instruments of influence even more aggressively than in the past.

This fear too seems overblown. It is most unlikely that Iran would actually employ nuclear weapons for any reason short of regime preservation, particularly because Iran will remain inferior to all the other nuclear powers more or less indefinitely. Given crushing U.S. superiority across the entire military (and economic and political) spectrum, there are many potential responses available to the United States short of forced regime change with which to deter or punish Iranian transgressions.

The recent revelation of alleged Iranian-sponsored attempts to assassinate the Saudi ambassador to the United States and attack the Israeli embassy there illustrates this proposition. Iran does not currently possess nuclear weapons, yet the U.S. government is not considering invading and occupying that country in reaction to this conspiracy. The expenses entailed in forced regime change in Afghanistan and Iraq effectively militate against attempting to do the same in a country three times more populous. If the Iranian leadership sanctioned this plot, it was not deterred by the huge U.S. nuclear arsenal, nor would the U.S. government be deterred from responding in turn if Iran had such weapons. Although Iran is most unlikely to employ nuclear weapons in circumstances short of defense of the regime, it might be tempted to adopt a more belligerent attitude in dealing with its neighbors and regional adversaries, particularly those without their own nuclear deterrent. For this reason, the United States will have to stand ready to supply a counterweight by extending its own nuclear umbrella over those friends and allies in the region that seek such assurances.

The United States has already begun to put in place one element of such extended deterrence by arranging to provide Europe with a shield against Iranian missile attacks. The United States has also collaborated closely with Israel on anti–ballistic-missile technology. As Iran moves toward a nuclear weapon capability, one will likely see similar U.S. support offered to other regional states.

Deploying defenses against Iranian nuclear attack involves what is called *deterrence by denial*—that is to say, physically denying the Iranians the capacity to conduct a successful attack. The United States is also likely to protect its friends and allies by extending deterrence by punishment—that is to say, retaliation. Given overwhelming U.S. military superiority, such a promise should represent a more credible form of deterrence than that which the United States extended over Cold War Europe. Then the United States had to promise to commit suicide in defense of its European allies. Cold War deterrence rested upon what was accurately referred to as *mutually assured destruction*. In the case of Iran, U.S. guarantees will rely instead on the promise of unilaterally assured destruction because only one side, the United States, will possess the power to destroy the other.

Sanctions

Sanctions and other forms of persuasion should be deployed for both long- and short-term purposes. The long-term objective should be to bring Iran fully into compliance with the NPT. The short-term objective should be to halt the Iranian program short of weaponization. Achievement of both objectives will require the deft employment of carrots and sticks. Carrots should be deployed if Iran agrees to verification measures that convincingly demonstrate that it has not weaponized, but with enough sticks retained to provide a continuing incentive to eventually bring that country, perhaps under new leadership, back into full conformity with the NPT.

Engagement

Diplomacy is unlikely to yield substantial breakthroughs as long as the current Iranian leadership remains in power. The United States nevertheless needs reliable channels of communication with the Iranian regime in order to garner information, signal warnings, avoid unintended conflict, and be positioned to move on openings toward accord when and if one arises. Should Iran actually build and deploy nuclear weapons, such channels of communication will become all the more important.

U.S. ambassadors in capitals and multinational posts, such as the UN, should be authorized to hold discussions with their Iranian counterparts within the framework of their existing responsibilities and instructions. These contacts should occur quietly and without fanfare. Eventually, if and when Tehran proves receptive, some privileged channel for more-comprehensive conversations could be established. The United States should negotiate an incidents-at-sea agreement with Tehran and set up other emergency channels for communication.

Soft Power

Regime change is the best—maybe the only—path to achieving all three main U.S. objectives. But explicit U.S. efforts to bring about such change, whether overt or covert, will probably have the reverse effect, helping perpetuate the regime and strengthen its current leaders. For the immediate future, therefore, the best thing the United States can do is to encourage political reform in Iran and other Middle Eastern countries where the United States has greater access and influence. Adopting a region-wide and, indeed, globally consistent approach to democratization is important to establishing the credibility of U.S. support for reform in Iran.

Soft power should be envisaged more as a magnet than as a lever. The best way of employing the attractive elements of U.S. society is simply to remove barriers to exposure. Making Internet censorship more difficult is one way of doing this. Facilitating travel, commerce, and study abroad is also important. Sanctions erect barriers to this kind of exposure. These barriers represent an unavoidable trade-off between the objectives of containment and the promotion of domestic reform, a

xxii   Coping with a Nuclearizing Iran

trade-off that needs to be carefully considered each time new sanctions are levied or old ones renewed.

Reformers in Iran are pressing for evolution, not revolution. The Green Movement is not seeking to overturn the Iranian constitution's unique mix of republican and Islamic elements but rather to give more reality to the former. Oddly enough, Ahmadinejad is challenging the status quo from the other end of the political spectrum. In the short term, neither the Green Movement nor Ahmadinejad seems likely to succeed. But Iran has a young, reasonably well-educated population, one increasingly plugged into the world around it. Even as the United States seeks to isolate and penalize Iran for its external misbehavior and nuclear ambitions, it should be seeking to maximize the exposure of its population to the United States, the West, and the newly dynamic Middle East. By the same token, the United States should avoid any association with separatist elements and extremist groups, whom the vast bulk of the Iranian people reject.

Acknowledgments

We would like to thank Marin Strmecki of the Smith Richardson Foundation for his support throughout this research. We would also like to thank Suzanne Maloney, Barry Blechman, and Larry Hanauer for their insightful and helpful reviews.

Abbreviations

ABM	anti–ballistic missile
AKP	Adalet ve Kalkınma Partisi
CISADA	Comprehensive Iran Sanctions, Accountability, and Divestment Act
CNOOC	China National Offshore Oil Corporation
EU	European Union
GCC	Cooperation Council for the Arab States of the Gulf
GDP	gross domestic product
GECF	Gas Exporting Countries Forum
IAEA	International Atomic Energy Agency
ILSA	Iran and Libya Sanctions Act
ISF	Iraqi security forces
LAF	Lebanese Armed Forces
LNG	liquefied natural gas
MKO	Mujahedin-e Khalq Organization
NATO	North Atlantic Treaty Organization
NIE	National Intelligence Estimate

NPT	Treaty on the Non-Proliferation of Nuclear Weapons
OPEC	Organization of Petroleum Exporting Countries
PA	Palestinian Authority
PJAK	Partiya Jiyana Azad a Kurdistanê, or Free Life Party of Kurdistan
Saudi Aramco	Saudi Arabian Oil Company
UAE	United Arab Emirates
UN	United Nations
UNHCR	United Nations High Commissioner for Refugees
UNSCR	United Nations Security Council resolution
WMD	weapons of mass destruction
WTO	World Trade Organization

CHAPTER ONE

Introduction

Although Iran poses one of the most-significant foreign policy challenges to U.S. interests in the Middle East, there are surprisingly few analyses of Iran that integrate the different facets of this challenge and formulate a comprehensive strategy toward this critical country. Although a plethora of studies have examined the nuclear issue or a particular policy instrument for dealing with it (e.g., engagement, sanctions, deterrence, or a military strike),[1] other aspects of the Iranian challenge, as well as the broader regional context, are often ignored. Comprehensive studies of Iran exist, including several by RAND authors, but none offers an integrative strategy that considers critical trade-offs and necessary sequencing. Moreover, many studies on the subject are either long term, assuming a world with a nuclear-armed Iran,[2] or extremely short term, focusing almost exclusively on how to stop Iran from acquiring such weapons.[3] Thus, a real gap exists in formulating a comprehensive U.S. strategy toward Iran in the medium term—that is, over the next five to ten years—one that does not begin or end when Iran acquires a nuclear weapon capability, that seeks to advance all the main U.S. interests, and seeks to harness all possible regional and global forces in its support.

Since the Iranian revolution in 1979, the United States has followed containment toward the Islamic Republic, with occasional, usu-

---

[1] Blechman, Brumberg, and Heydemann, 2010.

[2] Lindsay and Takeyh, 2010.

[3] Davis et al., 2011.

ally half-hearted efforts at engagement. Throughout this period, U.S. policy has generally developed in an incremental and tactical fashion, with bureaucratic and political considerations inhibiting strategic thinking within the government. Even nongovernmental policy studies are often, as just mentioned, narrow in focus and driven by the crisis of the day. As a result, U.S. policy on Iran tends to be largely reactive and lacking in strategic context and planning.

The United States needs a more effective strategy for Iran. Such a strategy should offer the prospect not just of halting and eventually reversing Iran's nuclear weapon program but also of moderating both Iran's external behavior and its internal politics. This strategy should employ all the elements of influence open to the United States and take fully into account the views and behavior of other regional and global powers. Finally, the strategy should allow for the dynamic nature of the U.S.-Iranian relationship and contain branches capable of dealing with possible developments, including the success or failure of efforts to halt Iran's nuclear program and a hardening or softening in the nature of the regime.

In an effort to develop such a strategy, we begin this study with an analysis of U.S. interests with respect to Iran and the policies historically adopted to advance them. We then take a similar look at Iranian interests and policies. Next, we turn to look at the interests and policies of the other countries in the region and of the more-distant powers that have potential influence on Iran. We then review the main instruments available to U.S. policymakers—diplomacy, economic sanctions, military and covert action, and the various elements of soft power—and we assess Iran's susceptibility to each. Against this as background, we examine the strategic alternatives available to the United States in dealing with Iran, including preemption, containment, deterrence, and engagement, from which we draw what we believe to be the optimal mix.

CHAPTER TWO

U.S. Interests, Objectives, and Strategies

The United States has three broad objectives with respect to Iran: to halt and eventually reverse its nuclear program, to restrain its external behavior, and to promote internal political reform. These objectives could be mutually reinforcing, in the sense that progress toward any one might advance the others, but they are also in tension, in that efforts toward one can and often do make the others harder to achieve. Thus, internal reform in Iran could moderate that country's external policies and slow its efforts to seek nuclear weapons, but visible U.S. efforts to promote such reforms will probably have the opposite effect as long as the current regime remains in place. Similarly, effective containment of Iranian external influence could further radicalize the regime and lead it to redouble its efforts to acquire a nuclear weapon capability.

Halting Iran's nuclear program has been regarded as the United States's most urgent objective for at least the past decade, but it is not necessarily the most important. Even a nonnuclear Iran is and could remain a disruptive force in the region. On the other hand, a nuclear-armed Iran under a regime that otherwise adheres to international norms, is at peace with its neighbors, and respects human rights might still encourage other potential proliferators but would otherwise be of much less concern.

As a practical matter, these objectives are unlikely to be achieved entirely in isolation. An Iran that agrees to abandon its nuclear ambitions is also likely to moderate its behavior toward its neighbors. An Iran that democratizes is likely to reexamine and eventually revamp its foreign and security policies for the better.

Unfortunately, as has been noted, even if the three basic objectives are compatible, the policies to advance them are not—at least not entirely. Sanctions, diplomatic pressure, and the use or threat of force designed to compel Iran to halt its nuclear program probably strengthen domestic support for the regime and almost certainly strengthen not only the regime's but also the general Iranian public's desire to achieve a nuclear weapon capability. The isolation of the Iranian populace, which is an unavoidable effect of international sanctions, retards progress toward domestic liberalization. Overt U.S. efforts to promote regime change and counter Iranian influence spur more repression and feed the regime anxieties that motivate its nuclear program and its disruptive external behavior. Covert U.S. efforts, real or imagined, have the same effect, stimulating regime paranoia and discrediting domestic opposition to it.

To note these tensions is not to argue for the abandonment of such efforts. All policies have costs as well as benefits. The proponents of any course of action tend to emphasize the former and ignore the latter. Good policy depends on acknowledging and seeking to balance such trade-offs.

For the first 20 years following the Iranian revolution of 1979, U.S. policy was largely focused on restraining Iran's external behavior. For the past decade, Iran's nuclear ambitions have increasingly dominated U.S. concerns. U.S. support for regime change also grew, to the point at which, in 2002 and again in 2003, Washington actually spurned offers from Tehran to cooperate on Afghanistan and Iraq and negotiate out other U.S./Iranian differences, including over its nuclear program.[1]

Long History of Mutual Grievances

The current state of hostility between the two countries is rooted in a long and very real series of reciprocal grievances, beginning with U.S. support for the 1953 coup that overthrew popularly elected Iranian

---

[1]   Dobbins, 2008.

Prime Minister Mohammad Mossadegh. Subsequent U.S. support for Iran's authoritarian and repressive monarch, Mohammad Reza Shah Pahlavi, created a deep sense of resentment toward the United States among Iranians that continues to affect U.S.-Iranian relations to this day.

Mossadegh's removal might have had some short-term benefits for the United States. The shah kept Iran, a Cold War strategic prize, firmly in the Western camp. Iran also served as a reliable bulwark against Soviet influence in the Middle East. The British withdrawal from the Persian Gulf in 1971 resulted in even closer U.S.-Iranian economic and military ties; the shah became the United States's "gendarme" in the Persian Gulf in exchange for U.S. technical assistance and advanced weaponry. U.S.-Iranian relations were not trouble free; the shah was suspect of U.S. motives and resented U.S. criticism of his domestic policies. Nevertheless, prerevolutionary Iran was viewed by the United States as an "island of stability" in an often-turbulent Middle East.[2]

The 1979 Iranian revolution transformed Iran from an important U.S. ally into a regional nemesis. Iran's revolutionary leaders, along with millions of ordinary Iranians, viewed the United States as the force behind the shah's long and repressive rule. Iran's seizure of the U.S. embassy and the taking of U.S. hostages engendered long-lasting U.S. hostility toward Iran. For the subsequent three decades, Iran evoked images of radicalism and terrorism in U.S. minds.

The state of hostility between the two has seldom turned into armed conflict. Throughout this period, the United States largely relied on sanctions, diplomatic pressure, and allied countries to blunt and contain Iranian influence in the Middle East. These efforts were largely successful due to several factors. The Iranian regime, already weakened by internal instability and insurgency, was attacked by Saddam Hussein's Iraq in 1980. The resulting eight-year-long war sapped Iran's energy and blunted efforts to "export" its revolution to the wider Middle East. The U.S. goal of containing Iran was aided by Arab fears of Iranian influence; the Cooperation Council for the Arab States of

---

[2] President Jimmy Carter used the "island of stability" phrase at a Tehran banquet in late 1977.

the Gulf (also known as the Gulf Cooperation Council, or GCC) was formed in 1981 as a response to the Iranian revolution, although, as will be seen, the GCC has not always bolstered U.S. efforts to isolate Iran. More than anything, the Islamic Republic's self-inflicted isolation, in addition to U.S. sanctions, has limited its ability to project power in the wider Middle East.

There have been instances of "proxy" and even direct military conflict between Iran and the United States. The Shi'a Lebanese group Hizballah, backed by Iran, bombed the U.S. embassy and Marine barracks in Lebanon in 1983, resulting in the death and injury of hundreds of Americans. The United States rendered support to Saddam in his conflict with Iran; U.S. provision of economic and military aid and subsequent U.S. military intervention in the conflict gave a substantial boost to Saddam's war efforts. Nevertheless, proxy conflict between Iran and the United States did not end all engagement; the Reagan administration authorized the sale of arms to Iran in 1985 in the hope of securing the freedom of U.S. hostages in Lebanon and empowering "moderates" within the Iranian regime.

Iran's targeting of Kuwaiti shipping in the Persian Gulf (in reaction to Kuwait's support for Saddam Hussein) led the United States to take military action against Iran through Operation Praying Mantis. An Iranian commercial plane, carrying 290 passengers and crew, was mistakenly shot down by the USS *Vincennes* in July 1988. This U.S. military involvement in the Iran-Iraq War might have contributed to Iran's acceptance of the United Nations (UN)–brokered ceasefire with Iraq in August 1988, but it also further embittered Iranian opinion.

Ups and Downs in the Relationship

It was Iraqi, not Iranian, aggression that drew the United States more deeply into the Persian Gulf in 1990 and has held it there ever since. Saddam's 1990 invasion of Kuwait and his subsequent defeat by the United States–led coalition helped Iran reduce its isolation. Technically neutral during the war, the Islamic Republic came to be seen as a lesser threat to the GCC, and Iranian-Arab relations improved significantly. The state of hostility between Iran and the United States continued, though it did not lead to outright military conflict. Iran's opposition to the Israeli-Palestinian peace process and support for Palestinian terrorist groups were obstacles to rapprochement between the two nations. Meanwhile, U.S. military forces in the region were largely focused on enforcing comprehensive UN sanctions on Iraq.

The United States pursued a policy of "dual containment" toward Iran and Iraq in the 1990s. This was not very demanding as long as Iran faced hostile neighbors to its west (Iraq) and east (Afghanistan). A key element of U.S. containment policy was the 1996 Iran and Libya Sanctions Act (ILSA) (Pub. L. 104-172, 1976), which penalized U.S. and foreign companies that invested in Iran's energy sector. ILSA (later known as the Iran Sanctions Act, Pub. L. 109-293, 2006), followed the bombing of the U.S. military facility at Khobar Towers by a Saudi Shi'a group linked to Iran's Revolutionary Guards.

Nevertheless, the United States also sought engagement with the Islamic Republic. Secretary of State Madeleine Albright's 2000 apology for the 1953 coup was a clear signal of U.S. reconciliation efforts.[3] Iranian President Mohammad Khatami's concept of a "dialogue among civilizations" and a desire for a more open Iran also contributed to the easing of tensions.

Khatami's presidency witnessed instances of cooperation between Iran and the United States. Iran played an important role in establishing the new Afghan central government after the Taliban's 2001 defeat. For its trouble, Iran found itself included, only a few weeks later, in the "axis of evil" proclaimed by President Bush in January 2002, in a speech that implicitly threatened preemptive military action to halt the Iraqi, Iranian, and Korean nuclear programs.[4] The Khatami government nevertheless persisted in offering cooperation on Afghanistan, proposing to help to train Afghan forces fighting the Taliban, an offer not taken up by the United States. Shortly after the U.S. invasion of Iraq, the Iranian regime passed to Washington an even more com-

---

[3] Albright, 2000.

[4] Bush, 2002.

prehensive offer to negotiate out all outstanding U.S.-Iranian differences. Again this initiative was ignored.[5]

U.S. lightning campaigns, first in Afghanistan and then in Iraq, removed Tehran's two nearest enemies but left the Iranian regime fearing that it might be next. The resultant combination of gratitude and fear helps explain the Iranian overtures of 2002 and 2003, while the hubris occasioned by these apparently easy victories helps explain the lack of interest these offers inspired in Washington. Soon thereafter, however, the United States became bogged down in inconclusive counterinsurgency campaigns in both countries, reducing Iranian fears of United States–promoted regime change. The mid-2003 Iranian overture for cooperation was not repeated. The 2005 election of Mahmoud Ahmadinejad as president opened a period of heightened confrontation between the two governments. Iran supported the United States–backed governments in both Afghanistan and Iraq but also aided militant groups targeting U.S. soldiers in both countries, principally Iraq, in order to keep the United States off balance and signal its capacity to do the United States even greater harm there if it chose.

The U.S. sanction regime against Iran has been greatly expanded in recent years in reaction to the Iranian nuclear program. Beginning in 2005, Iran has also been subjected to UN sanctions targeting its banking, energy, and military-industrial sectors. The Bush administration stated that military attacks on Iran's nuclear facilities are "not off the table," a threat Obama has neither withdrawn nor repeated.[6] Nevertheless, first the Bush and then the Obama administrations also pursued engagement with Iran through the P5+1.[7] Obama sent direct televised messages to the Iranian people and private messages to the Supreme Leader. Obama's overtures met little response and were largely discontinued after the 2009 Iranian presidential election and the regime's subsequent harsh crackdown on those protesting an allegedly fixed result.

---

[5]   Dobbins, 2008.

[6]   Klein, 2010.

[7]   Five permanent members of the UN Security Council (United States, China, Russia, United Kingdom, and France) plus Germany.

CHAPTER THREE

Iran's Interests, Objectives, and Strategies

The 2009 Iranian presidential election highlighted the social, economic, and political transformation of Iran. The election and its violent aftermath portended an increasingly militarized system of government potentially possessing nuclear weapons. Yet the world also witnessed the power of an emerging opposition movement cutting across all sectors of Iranian society. Although the Green Movement has not succeeded in changing the political system, it nevertheless has demonstrated a real desire for change in Iran and, perhaps, a better future for U.S.-Iranian relations. The transformation of U.S.-Iranian relations, however, is constrained by the bitter history between the two nations. Iranian suspicions of the United States run deep, though a sense of pragmatism and desire for reduced tensions pervades Iranian policymaking. Nevertheless, a marked improvement in ties between the two countries is unlikely as long as Khamenei remains in power. The rise of the principlists (fundamentalists) and the Revolutionary Guards might also lead to more-assertive Iranian behavior in the region and to growing tension and conflict between Iran and the United States in the near future.

A theocracy led by an effectively unelected and largely unaccountable Supreme Leader, the Islamic Republic has nevertheless possessed some characteristics associated with a democratic system of government—among them, regular parliamentary and presidential elections.[1] This provided Iranians with some limited say in the political system. However, the contested 2009 presidential election results weakened the "social contract" between the people and their rulers by failing to meet standard and acceptable levels of fairness and transparency.[2] The incumbent Ahmadinejad was declared the winner merely hours after the polls had closed, sparking allegations of fraud from his challengers, including former Prime Minister Mir Hussein Mousavi and millions of Mousavi's supporters.[3]

The election and its aftermath witnessed the marginalization of factions and personalities that had formed part of the fabric of the revolutionary state. Reformists led by such figures as Mousavi and Khatami were effectively sidelined from the political system; even former president Ayatollah Hashemi Rafsanjani, a founding father of the Islamic Republic, was threatened with arrest. The election and the subsequent violent crackdown also demonstrated the power of the Islamic Revolutionary Guards Corps, which arguably has become Iran's most powerful economic and political institution.

The election also complicated U.S. efforts to resolve the impasse over Iran's nuclear program. The Obama administration's policy of engagement with Iran was hindered by the chaos in Iran, by Washington's reservations about continuing to reach out to the regime even as millions of its citizens were protesting its legitimacy, and by the

---

[1] The Assembly of Experts, which is elected by the population, has the constitutional right to elect and supervise the Supreme Leader. However, assembly candidates must be approved by the conservative Guardian Council, which is beholden to Khamenei.

[2] It is perhaps impossible to tell who would have won the election if it had been held in a free and transparent manner. Mousavi appeared to be popular in urban areas, yet Ahmadinejad maintained a broad base of support throughout the countryside. It is possible that the election could have gone to a second round given each candidate's electoral strengths. On the other hand, Ahmadinejad's announced vote count was not inconsistent with some opinion polling conducted both before and after the elections (admittedly, not under ideal conditions). But the manner in which the government handled the election and rushed to announce its result led many Iranians, particularly Mousavi supporters, to perceive the entire election as fraudulent.

[3] Siamdoust, 2009. The early announcement of the results, in addition to the involvement of the pro-Ahmadinejad Ministry of Interior in supervising and certifying the results, led to wide claims of fraud. Also see Milani, 2009.

regime's inability or unwillingness to reach a consensus on a possible compromise solution. Nevertheless, the postelection Iranian government has not completely ruled out engagement or negotiations in solving the nuclear crisis. Ahmadinejad himself has appeared at times to be in favor of engagement and possible compromise. But the Iranian president is being marginalized by the regime—most notably, by the Supreme Leader.

Iranian Views of the United States

Iran's perception of the United States is greatly shaped by its self-image as a "subjugated" great power. Once the "super power" of its day, the Persian Empire stretched from North Africa to the Hindu Kush. A great conqueror, the Persian nation became prey to successive Greek, Arab, and Mongol invasions and eventually came under the domination of the British and Russian empires in the 19th century. The 1953 United States–planned overthrow of Mossadegh, who wrested Iran's oil industry from British control, and subsequent U.S. support for the repressive Pahlavi regime shaped Iranian perceptions of the United States as the region's new "imperial" power. This understanding of historical events is not only limited to the political elite but also appears to be shared by the Iranian public, particularly older generations.[4]

The Islamic Republic views the United States as its principal ideological and geopolitical enemy.[5] The Iranian elite, especially Khamenei, believe that the United States remains opposed to the revolution that overthrew the shah in 1979 and aims to replace an "independent" Islamic political system with that of a secular pro–United States regime, even if this is not explicitly advocated by the current U.S. administration. According to this viewpoint, U.S. hostility toward Iran is driven by cultural and ideological factors and the broader objective of keeping

---

[4]   Elson and Nader, 2011.

[5]   This view is shared by all factions across the political spectrum, although, as will be seen, there are major differences regarding Iran's policy toward the United States and allied nations.

the Middle East under U.S. control.[6] Hence, U.S. "interventions" in Iran's domestic affairs—such as moral (and, according to some Iranian officials, material) support for the Green Movement and the U.S. sanctioning of Iranian government officials responsible for the postelection crackdowns—constitute U.S. attempts to overthrow the Islamic Republic through a "velvet" revolution.[7] U.S. support and protection of Israel and the Arab states of the GCC are viewed as prolonging the U.S. "domination" of the Middle East and preventing Iran from assuming its role as the Persian Gulf's preeminent power.[8] Whereas the United States considers Iranian sponsorship of Hizballah, HAMAS, and others as support for terrorism, the Islamic Republic views ties to these groups as part of a strategy to prevent U.S. domination of Iran and the Muslim Middle East.

Iranian Factional Interests

Iran's political elite appear united in their view of the United States as the Islamic Republic's chief rival. Yet they are far from united on the extent of the U.S. threat and Iran's reaction to that threat. Each of the various factions, power centers, and personalities views the United States in a particular light. Each faction's control of the state apparatus has led to nuanced and, at times, relatively different policies toward the United States and its regional allies.

Iran's various factions often behave as political parties with corresponding constituents, policies, and ideologies. All factions fall under the umbrella of the Islamist political system; they are loyal to the revolution and its founder Ayatollah Ruhollah Khomeini and mostly accept *velayat-e faghih* (rule of the supreme jurisprudent), the political-ideo-

---

[6] For background on the Islamic Republic's strategic culture and views of the United States, see Thaler et al., 2010. Also see Takeyh, 2006.

[7] Hirshman, 2009. Increasing U.S. funding for democracy-promotion programs has driven the regime's perceptions of a "velvet revolution."

[8] Barzegar, 2010.

logical foundation for the clerical regime. Secular, leftist, and nationalist groups are prohibited from participating in the political system.

Iranian factions can be broadly divided into the traditional conservatives, the pragmatic conservatives, the principlists, and the reformists.[9] The first three factions, though on the right of the political spectrum, have distinct domestic and foreign policies. They adhere to the "ideals" of the revolution and espouse conservative views of religion and society; the traditional and pragmatic conservatives are closely tied to the bazaar and Iran's traditional business community. They are led by the "old men's" club of the Iranian revolution, which includes Khamenei and dozens of high-ranking clerics, whereas the principlists are composed of a younger generation hailing from the Revolutionary Guards and the Basij paramilitary forces. The traditional conservatives have strongly resisted political, economic, and social reforms they view as threatening revolutionary ideals and their own political and business prerogatives. They believe in the ideology of *moqavamat* (resistance) to the United States and the attainment of *khod-kafa i* (self-sufficiency). This has led to assertive foreign policies, such as active support for "resistance" groups (such as Hizballah), and Iran's uncompromising drive toward a nuclear weapon capability despite international sanctions and Iran's growing isolation.

The pragmatic conservatives, led by Rafsanjani, hold similar social and religious values, yet they believe in major economic (and, at times, political) reforms. Rafsanjani is a chief advocate for economic liberalization and privatization. As president from 1989 to 1997, he pursued foreign policies aimed at facilitating Iran's economic reconstruction after the devastation of the Iran-Iraq War.[10] The Islamic Republic, though still supporting such groups as Hizballah, refrained from "exporting" its revolution and stopped its subversion of the Persian Gulf's Sunni Arab regimes, though this did not prevent it from seeing itself as the region's premier power. Rafsanjani was also inclined to pursue a policy of détente with Europe and the United States, though his policies were often undermined by Iran's support for terrorist groups and its often-

---

[9]   Thaler et al., 2010. See also Buchta, 2000.

[10]   Ehteshami, 1995.

radical rhetoric.[11] Rafsanjani and the pragmatic conservatives were also constrained by Khamenei, who has the final say in foreign policy matters.

The principlists have emerged as Iran's most powerful political grouping, particularly after Ahmadinejad's 2005 election. Their rise has coincided with the ascent of the Revolutionary Guards, which, although not a monolithic organization, is nevertheless dominated by principlist officers. They are conservative, if not reactionary, in their cultural and political values. Many believe that the Islamic Republic has strayed from its true revolutionary "principles" under the leadership of Rafsanjani and Khatami. In their view, Iran's myriad political, economic, and security ills can be solved by a stricter enforcement of these principles. This has not prevented many of them, however, from taking command of Iran's economy and enriching themselves in the process.

The principlists also strongly believe that the Islamic Republic and the United States are locked in conflict over hegemony in the Middle East and beyond. Many perceive the United States to be in a state of decline, however, and see Iran as the region's ascendant power. Thus the principlists are less likely to compromise or be pressured on any issues shaping U.S.-Iranian relations, though more-pragmatic voices do exist among them.

The reformist movement has its origins in radical, left-leaning Islamic groups that overthrew the shah, took hostages at the U.S. embassy, helped create Hizballah, and sought to export the revolution to Arab states.[12] The most visible reformist leader today, Mir Hussein Mousavi, served as Khomeini's prime minister from 1980 to 1989, during which time he oversaw Iran's war with Iraq and the execution of thousands of Iranian dissidents. However, the reformist movement has undergone a significant transformation in the past two decades. The reformists have lost much faith in past economic and foreign policies

---

[11] The 1992 Mykonos assassinations of Iranian opposition leaders in Germany and Rafsanjani's direct involvement in the affair dampened Iranian-European rapprochement (Iran Human Rights Documentation Center, 2007).

[12] Sadr, 2010.

that emphasized the redistribution of wealth and the spread of the revolution. They believe that the Islamic Republic must implement fundamental reforms that will create a more viable political system in the face of Iran's myriad political, economic, social, and security problems. As president from 1997 to 2005, Khatami pursued foreign policies that eased Iran's international isolation and led to greater trade and foreign investment. Iran enacted a policy of détente with the GCC states, especially Saudi Arabia, and established relatively close ties with some European countries. Khatami, promoting a "dialogue of civilizations," also pursued engagement with the United States. Under his direction, the Islamic Republic played a critical role in defeating the Taliban and establishing the Karzai government in Afghanistan in 2001–2002.[13] In addition, Khatami's government engaged the European Union and the International Atomic Energy Agency (IAEA) on the nuclear program and ceased uranium enrichment in 2004 as a compromise gesture.[14]

The Green Movement, born after the 2009 presidential election, represents a broad spectrum of reformist groups, in addition to important sectors of Iran's civil society, including human and women's rights organizations.[15] Though led by Islamists, such as Mousavi, Khatami, and former Speaker of Parliament Mehdi Karroubi, the Green Movement also contains secular and nationalist elements.[16] It is not strictly a political faction, but the Green Movement nevertheless represents an important current in Iranian politics. The leaders of the Green Movement strongly believe in the revolution and the Islamic Republic, though they have emerged as equally strong opponents to the political status quo maintained by Khamenei and Ahmadinejad. They are also wary of the Guards' role in politics.

The Green Movement in power would likely pursue less strident foreign policies. Mousavi and others have strongly attacked Ahmadine-

---

[13] Dobbins, 2007. See also Dobbins, 2009.

[14] Kerr, 2004. However, it should be noted that Iran's cessation of enrichment could be interpreted as a political cover because the development of Iran's nuclear infrastructure continued unabated.

[15] For more on the Green Movement's support base, see Hashemi and Postel, 2010.

[16] Mohammadi, 2010.

jad over the handling of Iran's foreign policy, especially on the nuclear program.[17] Though the reformists support the nuclear program as Iran's inalienable right, they are nevertheless alarmed by Ahmadinejad's handling of nuclear policy vis-à-vis the United States and the international community. The Green Movement, along with pragmatic conservatives, such as Rafsanjani, has repeatedly warned that Ahmadinejad's nuclear policy will place Iran on a collision course with the United States. U.S. and international sanctions against Iran appear to have a greater impact on their thinking than on the traditional conservatives and the principlists.[18] This is due to the negative effect of sanctions on their key constituents—urbanized professional middle and upper classes, the young, and government technocrats—and their objectives of reforming Iran's political and economic system.

The Green Movement leadership might also see Iran's belligerent foreign policies, possibly even including support to armed "proxies," such as Hizballah and HAMAS, as endangering their own political and economic interests and even the very existence of the system they helped establish.[19] However, the Green Movement currently has minimal influence in shaping foreign policies ranging from the nuclear program to Iran's increasing support for "resistance" groups, such as Hizballah. The 2009 presidential election effectively pushed the reformists out of the political system and weakened the position of pragmatic conservatives, such as Rafsanjani. Barring unforeseen developments, Iran's policies in the next few years will be determined by the conservative Khamenei, in addition to principlist Revolutionary Guards officers.

Ideological Opposition to the United States

Supreme Leader Ayatollah Khamenei will have the final say in U.S.-Iranian relations. A conservative revolutionary tortured in the shah's

---

[17] Nasseri, 2009.

[18] Fassihi, 2010.

[19] "Iran Hardliners Condemn Khatami," 2008.

jails, Khamenei maintains a deep-rooted personal and ideological animosity toward the United States.[20] He has repeatedly denounced U.S. intentions toward Iran and has accused the United States of sponsoring a velvet revolution.[21] His replies to President Obama's speeches and letters have been far from positive. Nevertheless, Khamenei has also indicated that he is open to engagement with the United States if it benefits the Islamic Republic.[22] He has tolerated limited cooperation with the United States in the past, including Iran's help in establishing the Karzai government. Far from a rabid ideologue, Khamenei pursues pragmatic policies that appear to serve regime interests.

Khamenei's political and economic interests will nevertheless hinder any potential engagement with the United States. He leads a relatively closed political and economic system dependent on energy exports; political reform coupled with a more open economy could seriously weaken his authority among his conservative constituents. Hence, Khamenei has continuously opposed the reformists' sociopolitical agenda, which he views as threatening not only the ideals of the revolution but also his own personal authority. Khatami's election in 1997 came as a blow to Khamenei and his conservative supporters. The reformists' relatively liberal sociopolitical views and more-moderate foreign policies were viewed by them as a threat to the status quo. Reformist critiques of *velayat-e faghih* appeared to him as a direct threat to his authority.

The U.S. invasion and occupation of Afghanistan (2001) and Iraq (2003), combined with the reformist hold on the elected government, created a sense of siege for the Khamenei regime; Iran was fully encircled by a nemesis bent on creating a new Middle East. Iran's conciliatory behavior toward the United States after 9/11, the invasion of Afghanistan, and the invasion of Iraq reflected both a sense of threat and opportunity. However, the subsequent U.S. policy of regime change, Iran's inclusion in the "axis of evil," and Washington's spurning of Iranian offers of cooperation on Afghanistan and Iraq, in addi-

---

[20] Sadjadpour, 2008a.

[21] Khalaji and Clawson, 2009.

[22] Sadjadpour, 2008a.

tion to the opportunities offered Iran by the Afghan and Iraqi insurgencies, led Iran to adopt policies more hostile to the United States, such as providing significant military support to Iraqi Shi'a insurgents and more-limited support to Taliban elements.[23] The regime's internal and external vulnerabilities also contributed to the rise of Ahmadinejad and the Revolutionary Guards.

Ahmadinejad's election in 2005 was initially a boon for Khamenei.[24] The two men appeared to share an ideological outlook and a similar dislike of the reformist movement. Khamenei, who has become dependent on the principlists and Revolutionary Guards for political support, backed Ahmadinejad over his political opponents, including Rafsanjani and Khatami. Though not as powerful as Khamenei, Ahmadinejad became the face and voice of the Islamic Republic by virtue of his position as president and his consistent self-promotion. He pursued assertive policies at home and abroad, ranging from silencing opposition voices to reforming Iran's mammoth subsidy system and, of course, the continuation of the nuclear program in the face of international sanctions. Yet Ahmadinejad also indicated a willingness to engage and negotiate with the United States. This was reflected in his communications with President Obama and by his advocacy of the uranium "swap" deal, which fell apart after intense opposition at home.

Ahmadinejad is not a member of the traditional political elite, as are Khamenei and Rafsanjani, who led the revolution and created the Islamic Republic. A relative political novice, Ahmadinejad is closely associated with the Revolutionary Guards and the paramilitary Basij forces. He claims to have served in the Guards during the Iran-Iraq War and served as the governor of the northwestern province of Ardabil. Prior to being elected president in 2005, he served as Tehran's mayor. Ahmadinejad's 2005 victory came as a surprise to many Iranians; he was a "dark horse" running against Rafsanjani, one of the

---

[23] Nader and Laha, 2011.

[24] Ahmadinejad at first showed much-greater public respect and deference for Khamenei than his predecessors had shown, even kissing Khamenei's hand during his first presidential inauguration, for example. However, tensions greatly increased between the two in 2011 when Khamenei rejected Ahmadinejad's dismissal of the intelligence minister, sparking a major crisis between the president and the Supreme Leader.

most powerful men in the nation. However, the support of the Guards and the Basij and, more decisively, Khamenei, facilitated his election as president in 2005, and again in 2009.

Ahmadinejad positioned himself not only as a common man fighting the corrupt elite (i.e., Rafsanjani) but also as a force of resistance against "Western imperialism"—namely, the United States. He has also been a harsh and provocative critic of Israel. Under Ahmadinejad's government, Iran has provided deadly aid to anti–United States insurgents in Iraq and Afghanistan, increased military support to Hizballah and HAMAS, and continued Iran's nuclear weapon program. Nevertheless, Ahmadinejad has apparently sought some sort of compromise with the United States. Though ideological by nature, he might see some sort of détente as not only serving Iranian interests but also enhancing his position at home, claiming any type of "deal" with the United States as a personal victory.

The intense factional opposition to Ahmadinejad after the 2009 election has hindered any attempts at rapprochement with the United States. He nevertheless seems to have supported a swap deal that would have allowed Iran to ship a significant amount of its highly enriched uranium in exchange for fuel rods provided by Russia and France for Iran's medical research reactor. This potential compromise would have allayed Western fears about Iran's nuclear stockpile and allowed Iran to save face by keeping its uranium-enrichment capability. However, the deal came under intense criticism by Ahmadinejad's opponents, including Rafsanjani and Mousavi. Khamenei might well have also expressed his disapproval with the deal, although there is not much direct evidence of him having done so.

Ahmadinejad's public dispute with the Supreme Leader in 2011 has greatly diminished his standing among the political elite. His dismissal of Intelligence Minister Heidar Moslehi was countermanded by Khamenei, who commanded that Moslehi stay on in his post. Ahmadinejad's subsequent absence from cabinet meetings for ten days was viewed as a snub to the Supreme Leader and a direct challenge to his authority. Ahmadinejad's consistent support for his in-law and close adviser, Esfandar Rahim Mashaei, has also increased opposition to him from within the principlist camp. Mashaei, a proponent of "Iranian"

Islam (nationalism) and messianic notions, is viewed with great suspicion by the Iranian clergy. Mashaei has also been rumored to favor engagement with Washington, perhaps reflecting renewed interest by Ahmadinejad in such contacts. Ahmadinejad's support for Mashaei has resulted in severe criticism by the clergy and even senior figures within the Revolutionary Guards. Public scolding by Khamenei and the Guards might have, in effect, made him a lame duck for the remainder of his presidential term. This not only will affect his ability to shape domestic politics but also will make Iran even less likely or able to engage the United States on the nuclear issue.

The Revolutionary Guards

Established in the early years of the revolution to protect the Islamic Republic from internal and external threats, the Revolutionary Guards have become Iran's chief economic, political, and military powerbroker (with the exception of Khamenei himself). Ahmadinejad's election in 2005 (and again in 2009) cemented the Guards' hold on the political system and neutralized the reformists as a direct threat to the Supreme Leader.[25]

The Guards have arguably become the most powerful economic actor in Iran. The Guards' construction company Khatam al Anbia and numerous businesses operated by former officers have come to dominate major sectors of the Iranian economy, including the energy sector, telecommunications, transportation, construction, and even auto-making.[26] The Ahmadinejad government has awarded Khatam al Anbia hundreds of no-bid contracts, and the organization has assumed a major role in developing Iran's energy sector.[27] The Guards' enormous

---

[25] After the 1999 student riots, the Guards warned Khatami of a possible coup if he did not rein in the student protestors. In addition, serial murders of reformist intellectuals and activists by Iran's Ministry of Intelligence served as a warning to those who wanted to change the political system.

[26] Wehrey, Green, et al., 2009.

[27] Wehrey, Green, et al., 2009.

economic and financial power has eclipsed other key business and political players. Iran's various *bonyads* (foundations), which control large segments of the economy, are heavily influenced by the Guards.[28] Iran's traditional business elite, including the very wealthy Rafsanjani family, have seen their business influence and holdings challenged by Iran's new Guards elite.[29]

The Guards' economic weight has led to immense political and military power. Today, the Revolutionary Guards view themselves as not only the guardian of the revolution but also the interpreter and enforcer of its principles. The reformists, pragmatic and traditional conservatives, and even some principlists are viewed by Guards hard-liners as being unqualified for political office. The Guards and the subordinate Basij paramilitary forces played a crucial role in Ahmadinejad's election in 2005 and again in 2009. Before the election, Khamenei's representative to the Guards, Yadollah Javani, stated that Mousavi and the reformists were a threat to the Islamic Republic and would be "snuffed out" by the Guards.[30] The Guards also hold the key to Ahmadinejad's undoing.

The Guards have played the leading role in crushing the postelection protests, challenging or dominating various organizations responsible for internal security, such as the Law Enforcement Forces and the Ministry of Intelligence.[31] The Guards have also overshadowed the Artesh, Iran's conventional armed forces. Operational control of the Persian Gulf was transformed from the Artesh navy to the Guards in 2007. Iran's foreign policies in Iraq and Afghanistan are handled by the Guards' specialized Qods Forces. The Guards also control Iran's ballistic-missile forces and are likely to take command of Iran's potential nuclear weapon forces.

Of course, the Revolutionary Guards are hardly a monolithic force; divisions that afflict Iranian society and the political system are

---

[28] Wehrey, Green, et al., 2009.

[29] Bremmer, 2010.

[30] Erdbrink, 2009.

[31] Daragahi, 2009.

reflected within the force. Many Guards members are reported to support Mousavi and the reformists; others favor more-pragmatic principlists, such as Tehran mayor Mohammad-Bagher Qalibaf, a possible candidate in the next presidential elections.[32] Furthermore, some Guards appear to be unhappy with the handling of the 2009 election and its aftermath and might resent Ahmadinejad and Khamenei. Nevertheless, the Guards will probably be controlled by principlist officers in the near future. General Ali Jafari, commander-in-chief of the Revolutionary Guards, is a stalwart principlist loyal to Khamenei and the *velayat-e faghih*. Other high-ranking officers share a similar outlook.

The Guards' economic, political, and military power gives the Guards a decisive say in Iran's approach toward the United States. Top principlist members of the Guards are less likely to support a rapprochement with the United States. Their political outlook is shaped by fundamentalist ideology, and they view the United States as a geopolitical and cultural threat to the Islamic Republic. In addition, many top members of the Guards appear to share the ruling elite's view of the United States as a declining global power.[33] This has been shaped by the U.S. difficulties in Iraq, Afghanistan, and the U.S. financial crisis. Moreover, principlists within the Guards have been emboldened by the fall of Saddam Hussein, the Islamic Republic's chief regional rival, and the rise of the Shi'a in Iraq. Hizballah's military performance in its 2006 war with Israel, in addition to growing Iranian military capabilities, has also led to a sense of confidence among Guards principlists.[34] The Guards have repeatedly depicted the 2011 Arab uprising as a win for the Islamic Republic.[35]

Although the Guards are vulnerable to sanctions, their access to energy revenues and their role in running Iran's underground economy insulate them from the consequences more than either Green Move-

---

[32] Zand-Bon, 2010; Esfandiari, 2010.

[33] Majidyar, 2009.

[34] "U.S. Not in a Position to Attack Iran," 2010.

[35] "Azadi Qods Qafelgir Konand e Ast," 2011.

ment supporters or the pragmatic conservatives.[36] It is possible that some Guards elements might favor engagement with the United States from a position of strength, but ideological considerations and the political costs of "appeasing" the United States might prevent significant compromise and cooperation.

The Guards and the principlists are likely to play the biggest role in shaping Iranian foreign policy in the next five years. The reformists and Green Movement have been portrayed by the regime as enemies of the Islamic Republic and will be prevented from playing a large role in the political system. Pragmatic conservatives, such as Rafsanjani, have also been sidelined. The political status quo is likely to continue in the absence of major changes, such as a popular revolution or Khamenei's death, and, although Ahmadinejad's presidential term ends in 2013, it is unlikely that the next Iranian president will be able or willing to fundamentally reshape Iran's policies toward the United States and regional allies. The next Iranian president will more likely be a conservative, though he might be more pragmatic and less flamboyant than Ahmadinejad. However, even more-pragmatic principlists, such as Ali Larijani, current Speaker of Parliament and one of Ahmadinejad's chief critics, would probably not reshape Iranian foreign policy significantly. Larijani has stated that his differences with Ahmadinejad are a matter of "style, approach, and management" rather than substance or ideology.[37] He seems unlikely to change Iran's stance on the nuclear program or U.S.-Iranian relations if elected president.

Yet given the dramatic changes under way in the Arab Middle East, external circumstances could yield changes in Iranian foreign (and domestic) policy that cannot at this point be foreseen. On the one hand, democratization of several Arab states might leave Iran further isolated and subject to internal pressures for liberalization. Yet it is also possible that Iran's relationship with such states as Egypt could actually improve, as it already has with Iraq and Afghanistan, leaving the regime in Tehran less anxious about encirclement. Whether that less-

---

[36] See Wehrey, Green, et al., 2009; and Dehghanpisheh, 2010.

[37] Moubayed, 2008.

ened sense of isolation would lead to more-radical or moderate policies is hard to tell.

Iran's Future Nuclear Posture

Iran's nuclear program began under the shah's reign with U.S. assistance but was halted after the revolution due to lack of resources during the Iran-Iraq War. The Islamic Republic restarted the program in 1989, focusing on the construction of the nuclear plant in Bushehr in addition to the development of a uranium-enrichment capability. By the 1990s, evidence had emerged that Iran was pursuing not only a civilian nuclear capability but also a nuclear weapon capability. The revelation of secret sites at Natanz and Arak in 2002 heightened international concerns of an Iranian nuclear weapon program.

The Iranian nuclear program has achieved some notable successes since 2002. Iran has installed up to 8,000 centrifuges at the underground Natanz facility, though only about 5,000 might be operational.[38] Iran has also enriched uranium up to 20 percent, making it easier to create bomb-grade material at 90 percent. Given this capability, Iran has enough nuclear material to create about two nuclear bombs, provided it has mastered the creation of an actual nuclear device and a delivery mechanism.[39] Nevertheless, the U.S. intelligence community assesses Iran to be several years away from having the actual capability to create a functioning nuclear weapon.

Iran's pursuit of a nuclear weapon capability is primarily motivated by regime survival.[40] Iran's conventional military capabilities are no match for U.S. military might; the speedy U.S. overthrow of the Taliban in 2001 and Saddam Hussein in 2003 demonstrated the regime's vulnerability. U.S. failure to do anything comparable about North Korea underscores the utility of a nuclear deterrent. Iran might

---

[38] Clapper, 2011.

[39] Daragahi, 2010.

[40] For a more comprehensive explanation of Iran's nuclear motivations, see Davis et al., 2011.

have initially slowed its nuclear program after the U.S. invasion of Iraq; however, Ahmadinejad's presidency has seen a steady, if slow, development of Iran's capabilities. Though reassured by the U.S. preoccupation with the Iraqi and Afghan insurgencies, the Iranian regime nevertheless continues to fear regime change at U.S. hands.

In addition to regime survival, the Islamic Republic wishes to be viewed as the Middle East's preeminent power. The regime might perceive nuclear weapon capability as enhancing its prestige as the leader of the Muslim world, although Pakistan will certainly retain the lead in nuclear capability far into the future. An Iranian nuclear weapon capability could also help counter the influence of regional adversaries, such as Saudi Arabia. Iran is also worried about an increasingly unstable nuclear Pakistan threatened by fundamentalist Sunni groups hostile to Shi'a Iran.

Iran's experience during its war with Iraq might have informed its decision to pursue a nuclear weapon capability. Its political and military isolation after the revolution allowed Saddam Hussein to launch a massive attack on its territory, followed by ballistic-missile attacks on its cities and chemical weapon attacks on its forces in the field. Nuclear capability would almost certainly deter a potential regional adversary from launching a similar attack on Iran in the future.

Iran's pursuit of a nuclear civilian and even military capability is also a matter of pride. The Islamic Republic continually emphasizes *khod-kafai* (self-sufficiency) as one of its primary objectives. Advancement in all scientific fields, including nuclear technology, highlights the regime's progress in the face of "world arrogance" (the United States). Ahmadinejad, beset by domestic opposition and a declining economy, has, in particular, identified his presidency with the nuclear program's success.

The regime in Tehran denies any intention of developing nuclear weapons, claiming these to be immoral. Public opinion polling nevertheless indicates that Iranians increasingly favor such a course.[41] There are also multiple technical indications that Iran is pursuing a nuclear weapon capability. One might question why Iran has chosen to pursue

---

[41] Elson and Nader, 2011.

such a confrontational approach toward Israel, the United States, and its Arab neighbors, but, having done so, it would seem almost inconceivable that Iran would not seek the protection a nuclear deterrent could afford.

The Iranian regime thus has ample incentive to acquire a nuclear weapon capability, and it has adequate technical capacity to do so. Despite mounting economic sanctions, there seems little inclination, among either Iranian elites or the general public, to abandon this goal. How far to take it, however, might still be an open question. Iran could choose to maintain a virtual capability, meaning that it possesses the know-how and the necessary materials to develop a nuclear weapon, but to not proceed to manufacture, assemble, and test them. This is sometimes referred to as the *Japanese option* because that country is believed to possess such capabilities. Alternatively, Iran could build but neither test nor acknowledge its possession of nuclear weapons, which is usually termed the *Israeli option*. Lastly, it could test and openly acknowledge deployment of such weapons, the North Korean option.

Governments tend not to make difficult or controversial decisions until they have to do so, so it is plausible that the Iranian leadership has not yet decided how far to take Iran's nuclear program. Even if it has so decided, it is at least theoretically possible to persuade the leadership to halt at any one of those thresholds. The Iranian regime's ultimate nuclear posture will be shaped by internal and external factors. Although there is broad elite and popular support for the civilian nuclear program, there is also evidence to suggest significant divisions over how far to go.[42] In particular, reformist and pragmatic conservative factions are most likely to oppose weaponization because Iran's resulting isolation would damage their political and reformist agendas. This does not mean that the reformist and pragmatic conservatives would forgo a nuclear weapon capability completely. Rather, they would weigh the costs and benefits carefully and not view a weapon capability as an ultimate objective.

The principlists and the Revolutionary Guards, however, have based their legitimacy in part on the success of the nuclear program.

---

[42] Miller and Warrick, 2011.

A declared nuclear capability could enhance their legitimacy among the elite and the Iranian population. Nevertheless, even the principlists and the Guards will consider the costs and benefits of nuclear weaponization because the world's reaction to a nuclear-armed Iran could potentially damage their long-term interests in survival and power accumulation.

The regime is also susceptible to international pressure, especially sanctions. It is unlikely to weaponize its nuclear program if it thinks that doing so would undermine the regime's longevity. A demonstrated or declared capability would further alienate Iran from its neighbors and the international community, including close commercial partners, such as China. In addition, openly abandoning the Treaty on the Non-Proliferation of Nuclear Weapons (NPT) could invite a U.S. or Israeli military strike and encourage acquisition of nuclear weapons by Iran's Arab neighbors.

For these reasons, a virtual nuclear capability in which Iran maintains the ability to create weapons might best suit the regime's interests. Iran would limit international pressure by appearing to remain within the bounds of the NPT while maintaining the capability to create a nuclear deterrent. The Islamic Republic could weaponize its program if it felt that it was coming under threat of invasion or regime change, or even after an armed attack by Israel or the United States.

Conclusion

The achievement of U.S. objectives toward Iran will be shaped by several major factors. Chief among them is a deep-seated hostility toward the United States formed by historical grievances and Iranian nationalism. In addition, members of the Islamic Republic's ruling elite, including Ayatollah Khamenei and principlists within the Guards, are ideologically and politically opposed to a rapprochement with the United States. Khamenei and the Guards are more resistant to pressures, such as sanctions. U.S. and UN sanctions have undoubtedly hurt the Iranian economy and limited Iran's capacity to project military power, but it is not clear whether they will be able to shape Iranian decisions on the nuclear program. It is possible that sanctions and Iran's international isolation have put greater pressure on factions and personalities opposed to Ahmadinejad and the status quo. These include the Green Movement and pragmatic conservatives who view the militarization of politics and Iran's confrontation with the United States and allies with great alarm. They are also more susceptible to a policy of engagement and pressure that could dissuade Iran from further advancing or weaponizing its nuclear program. However, the 2009 presidential election and its aftermath have marginalized these groups in favor of the principlists within the Revolutionary Guards.

The principlists view Iran as the Middle East's ascendant power. Nevertheless, such a sense of confidence, whether realistic or not, is unlikely to dramatically reshape Iran's policies toward the United States and its regional allies. Iranian foreign policy since Khomeini's death in 1989 has been defined by a sense of pragmatism and caution, though the enmity with the United States still remains.

The Islamic Republic's chief objective is the survival of a regime that has held power for more than 30 years. Khamenei and his supporters view the suppression of internal dissent as the best means to maintain the status quo. They also appear to view Iran's nuclear capability as the best means to ensure regime survival against the U.S. military threat. Hence, they might be willing to bear the costs of Iran's nuclear drive as long as these do not overwhelm the regime. The status quo—an increasingly authoritarian regime and hostility toward the United States short of war—suits Khamenei and the Guards' interests. Recent popular uprisings throughout the Arab Middle East might eventually affect Iranian calculations and, perhaps, Iranian domestic politics; however, at this point, abandonment of the quest for a nuclear weapon capability and any substantial improvement in U.S.-Iranian relations seems unlikely in the absence of some significant change in the Iranian system of government.

CHAPTER FOUR

The Other Actors

Washington and Tehran are locked into a confrontation that, although it might not lead to actual collision, seems unlikely to ease as a result of initiatives from either capital. On the other hand, the region surrounding Iran is undergoing dramatic change. The long-term outcomes of the wars in Iraq and Afghanistan are unclear, as are the effects of the Arab Spring on neighboring regimes, not to speak of that in Tehran itself. U.S. interests vis-à-vis Iran are largely derivative of its ties to these nearby states, and the success of any strategy is dependent on their support.[1]

---

[1] We have chosen to examine several states that we deem to be most critical in having the ability to affect Iranian policies in the midterm time frame. We select states over which the United States is assumed to have leverage, either because they are close U.S. partners with extensive political and security relationships (Israel, Saudi Arabia and the GCC, Turkey) or because Western political and economic levers might affect the extent of their alignment with Iran (Syria). We also consider extraregional actors, such as China, Russia, and the European Union, given their extensive economic relations with Iran and their role in the UN Security Council, which is critical to the U.S. sanction efforts. Egypt is a leading regional state that we do not consider in depth because its ability to affect the three main U.S. policy goals has been limited in the past and because its recent revolution is likely to lead to a continued focus on internal developments. Although a post-Mubarak Egypt might renew that nation's diplomatic relationship with Iran, it will hold few political or economic levers over the next several years to dramatically assist or undermine the Iran policy goals of the United States. The same can be said for other important, albeit smaller, regional partners, such as Jordan, which are also facing mounting domestic unrest.

The Gulf Cooperation Council States

At first glance, the views of the Gulf states toward Iran would appear to align neatly with those of the United States, insofar as they all view Iran as their principal security threat. But some feel that threat more acutely than others do. The toppling of Saddam in 2003 and the rise to power of Iraqi Shi'a were cataclysmic events that removed a long-standing Arab and Sunni "buffer" against Persian and Shi'a influence.[2] These developments coincided with the ascent of Ahmadinejad and the principlists in Tehran, who adopted a strident and patronizing air toward the Gulf states that stood in stark contrast with the conciliatory tone of the Khatami era.[3] Iran's meddling in Iraq, and especially its lethal support to Shi'a militias, drew widespread condemnation from Gulf governments and closer alignment with the United States.[4] The result was an increased GCC dependence on U.S. protection, but also a trend in security diversification—some of these governments also sought greater support from Russia, France, and China to supplement U.S. power, spurred by the perception of U.S. entanglement in Iraq. The Gulf states fear that an Iranian nuclear capability could embolden that regime in its efforts to project influence throughout this region by subversion, propaganda, support for terrorism, and even outright aggression while diminishing U.S. capability or willingness to bring countervailing pressures to bear.[5]

Yet, beneath this narrative of alarmism—and the appearance of consensus with the United States—Gulf policies toward Iran are actually more nuanced and divergent than immediate impressions suggest.[6] Despite their concerns, the Gulf states possess neither the will nor the capacity to act in complete unison with U.S. strategy toward Iran, whether this entails containment, military action, or engagement, instead exhibiting the following:

---

2   For a representative view, see al-'Abideen ar-Rukabi, 2008.

3   For background, see Gasiorowski, 2007.

4   Al-Dayni, 2007.

5   For background, see Wehrey and Kaye, 2010.

6   For overviews of Gulf dilemmas, see Partrick, 2008, and Shanahan, 2009.

- *A preference for hedging.* There is a strong inclination in the Gulf for hedging on Iran, i.e., preserving at least a modicum of communication, trade, and cultural ties. This is partly due to concern about swings in U.S. policy, but also because the Gulf states acknowledge Iran as a neighbor with which they must coexist, while the United States, despite its massive presence and military infrastructure in the Gulf, is seen as an ultimately transitory power.

- *Intra-Gulf disunity.* The GCC is hardly united in its approach toward Iran; there are sharp distinctions between the alarmist views of Saudi Arabia and Bahrain and the more-accommodating stances of Oman and Qatar. In many cases, Oman and Qatar have adroitly exploited the Iran threat to balance and irritate Saudi Arabia, whose aspirations for GCC leadership are frequently viewed as heavy handed. Although Doha and Muscat could be problematic "gaps" in an anti-Iranian bloc, they are also helpful intermediaries and interlocutors for the United States.

- *Differences in threat perception.* There is an oft-overlooked divergence between how Washington and the Gulf states perceive the threat from Iran. For the GCC, Iran's principal threat lies not in its conventional military capability (although its ballistic missiles and naval capabilities are certainly worrisome), or even the danger of a direct nuclear attack. Rather, the threat is an asymmetric and ideological one—its efforts to seize the moral high ground on the Palestine issue, its support for regional militancy by HAMAS and Hizballah, its potential ability to mobilize disenfranchised Shi'as, and its existence as a socially conservative alternative to hereditary monarchy. The 2011 revolt in Bahrain has only intensified these fears, with Bahraini and Saudi officials making repeated and largely unsubstantiated accusations of Iranian and Hizballah incitement and material support to Bahraini Shi'as.[7] Although some Iranian support might have been possible, the fever pitch of Bahraini and Saudi rhetoric on Iran is likely intended to deflect attention from what is essentially a home-grown revolt, born of

---

[7] Solomon, 2011.

growing frustration at Bahrain's authoritarian government and economic disparities between the dominant and richer Sunnis and the more-numerous and much-poorer Shi'a. The Saudi military intervention in Bahrain was likely intended as a deterrent against Iran exploiting the Bahraini unrest and a visible reassertion of Saudi influence in the midst of the Arab world's tumult. It does nothing to mitigate the underlying roots of the revolt and, in fact, might be fueling increased radicalization among the Bahraini Shi'a, which might offer greater openings for Iranian influence.

- *Ambivalence about a military strike.* The Gulf states are highly conflicted about a U.S. or Israeli strike on Iran: They would certainly like to see Iran chastened and its potential nuclear capability destroyed, but they are also worried about Iran's retaliatory response via terrorism, the closure of the Hormuz Strait, potential environmental consequences, an Iranian ballistic-missile strike on both U.S. facilities and their own infrastructure, and, perhaps most of all, the reactions of their own populations to such an unprovoked attack.[8]

- *Wariness about human rights and democratization.* Although Gulf regimes are concerned about the assertive policies of the principlists in Tehran, they are equally alarmed about the prospect of successful democratization in Iran that could inspire similar demands for political reform among their own publics. Many of the Gulf regimes greeted the contested 2009 elections and subsequent crackdown with a muted, if not hostile, attitude toward the Green Movement.[9] This concern has intensified after the Arab revolutions that have shaken North Africa, Yemen, and Bahrain. As little as the Gulf regimes like a conservative theocracy in Iran, they probably fear a secular democracy even more. In this respect, their preferences are diametrically opposed to those of the United States.

---

[8]   Kaye and Wehrey, 2007; Henderson, 2005; El-Hokayem and Legrenzi, 2006; "Iran Tuhadid Duwal al-Khalij al-Muta'awinah ma' America bil Sawarikh," 2007.

[9]   For background, see Black, 2009.

- *Fear of U.S.-Iranian collusion.* Finally, several Gulf states, particularly Saudi Arabia, have been fearful of an eventual U.S.-Iranian rapprochement, which would deprive them of the privileged position they have enjoyed in the United States–backed security order for more than two decades.[10] The disclosure of the alleged Iranian plot to assassinate the Saudi ambassador to the United States— whether valid or not—could be a boon for the Saudis. It helps repair the previously rocky relationship with the United States, casts the kingdom as the victim, and refocuses Washington's attention back toward the containment of Iran, rather than the Arab Spring. It will also have a galvanizing effect on the GCC, hardening its already confrontational position toward Iran.

Saudi Arabia's perceptions of Iran as a strategic rival and ideological competitor make it a seemingly natural partner for a U.S. approach that aims to counter Iranian influence in the region. But there are significant limitations and liabilities inherent in the partnership that must be taken into account. The most crucial and recent example is Riyadh's reaction to the Arab revolts of 2011 and, in particular, its displeasure at what it perceived as the U.S. abandonment of Egyptian president Hosni Mubarak. Riyadh's subsequent behavior in the region has been focused on managing and, in some cases, rolling back the Arab revolts, such as its intervention in Bahrain. In addition, the Saudi leadership appears to perceive that any loosening of the status quo will result in a net gain for Iran—an exaggerated perception of threat that plays into the hands of the Islamic Republic and puts Riyadh at odds with Washington's attempts to encourage measured and peaceful reform in the region. Aside from this divergence, there are other areas of potential disagreement and friction regarding Iran:

- *Iraq.* Saudi Arabia's preference for a Sunni-dominated Iraq puts it at odds with both the United States and Iran. Saudi Arabia views Iraq as a contested arena in its larger geostrategic rivalry

---

[10] "Trilateral Talks Rattle Gulf States While Concealing Complex Iranian Dynamics," 2007; Stracke, 2009.

with Iran—political gains by Shi'a groups (and for democracy) are viewed as a win for Iran and a net loss for Riyadh. Riyadh's previous warnings that it will increase its involvement in Iraq to defend Sunnis following a U.S. departure should not be dismissed, but its role in containing Iranian power in Iraq might be more limited than is realized. In addition, Saudi Arabia is likely to adopt a degree of dialogue with Iran about maintaining order in a post-drawdown Iraq, which would be beneficial for U.S. interests. However, a key priority for Riyadh is to keep the United States closely involved in Iraq's security affairs, both as a buffer against Iran and as a check against a resurgent Iraqi military.[11]

- *The Levant.* In the Levant, U.S. and Saudi opposition to Iran's support for HAMAS and Hizballah intersect, but Washington should be similarly mindful of the risks of overreliance on Riyadh to counter the influence of these groups. Lebanon and, to a lesser extent, Gaza have witnessed a vigorous Saudi attempt to roll back Iranian influence using humanitarian aid, investment, media, and other soft power. In response to uprisings in Syria, Saudi Arabia has called for the removal of the Assad regime—a shift from its previous policy of trying to coax Assad out of Iran's orbit and back into the Arab fold. Although Riyadh is uneasy about endorsing the fall of another Arab leader in the midst of the Arab Spring and fears the spillover effect of a Syrian civil war, it likely sees the ouster of Assad as a major victory in its long-standing strategic struggle with Tehran. In these areas, Saudi Arabia sees an opportunity to regain the regional legitimacy and leadership it lost in Iraq. In Lebanon, Saudi Arabia feels a particular obligation to protecting local Sunnis, given its long-standing ties to the late prime minister, Rafik Hariri, and Lebanon's Salafis. In addition, King Abdallah achieved surprising success in repairing Saudi relations with Syria's Bashar al-Asad—a move that was at least partly calculated to encourage greater Syrian control in Lebanon

---

[11] Gause, 2007. Saudi preoccupation with Iraq achieved considerable notoriety with the publication of an op-ed by a semi-official analyst; see Obaid, 2006. The debate over Saudi intervention is covered in Stack, 2006, and Al-Humayd, 2007, 2008.

as a counterweight to Iran's growing influence.[12] On the Palestine issue, King Abdallah has advanced peace initiatives as a means to undercut Iran's rejectionism and the militancy of HAMAS and Hizballah. The Levant has also witnessed a modicum of Saudi-Iranian cooperation to prevent an escalation of violence by those nations' respective local allies.[13]

- *The Iranian nuclear program.* Saudi Arabia views Iran's nuclear program from multiple perspectives: as a potential existential threat, as an enabler of Iranian militancy across the region (both in the Levant and among Gulf Shi'a), as a coercive tool in Gulf diplomacy, and as an affront to Saudi leadership in the Islamic world.[14] Whether this would cause Riyadh to develop a comparable capability, on its own or in cooperation with Pakistan, is unknowable at this point. Such a step would signal a drastic break with its principal security patron, the United States, thus upending more than 50 years of fruitful cooperation, and would not be embarked upon lightly. Yet, depending on the assurances it receives from Washington, this is a risk that Riyadh might be willing to take. For now, Saudi leaders are supporting a variation of the U.S. approach, calling for a nuclear-free zone in the Persian Gulf—a departure from its previous insistence on a weapons of mass destruction (WMD)–free Middle East that implicitly included Israel. Nevertheless, the United States must account for the possibility that Riyadh could pursue a more unilateral path.[15]
- *Energy and financial levers.* Given its petroleum assets and prominent role in the Organization of Petroleum Exporting Countries (OPEC), Saudi Arabia possesses unique levers that can potentially aid the United States in pressuring or isolating Iran. However, many of these options are more limited than commonly assumed. First, U.S. officials appear hopeful that Riyadh's energy resources

[12] Worth, 2010a.

[13] Middle East Media Research Institute, 2007; Naïm, 2007; Blanford, 2007.

[14] "Al-Mashru' al-Irānī al-Iqlīmī wa al-Nawawī," 2009.

[15] For background on Saudi nuclear ambitions, see Bahgat, 2006.

will be leveraged on China (which counts Riyadh as its biggest supplier of oil) to solicit Beijing's support for tougher UN sanctions.[16] According to this line of thinking, Saudi Arabia could offer China better commercial opportunities in the petroleum sector than it currently finds in Iran. However, many analysts have downplayed this idea, citing differences between Beijing and Riyadh over joint-venture Saudi Arabian Oil Company (Saudi Aramco) refineries in China and Riyadh's desire to maintain a monopoly in oil exploration.[17] Similarly, it is unlikely that Riyadh would use its excess production capacity (estimated at 4 million barrels per day) to depress oil prices, constrict Iran's cash flow, and undermine the Iranian regime's ability to satisfy an already discontented population. Most significantly, this option ignores Riyadh's historical preference for maintaining solidarity with fellow OPEC members and, as noted earlier, its desire to avoid overtly provoking Iran for fear of Iranian retaliation.[18] Finally, the Saudi regime's hasty announcement of $35 billion in subsidies to placate domestic dissent in the wake of the Arab revolts creates a significant budgetary constraint on the regime's ability to deploy the "oil weapon." However, faced with the imminent prospect of an Iranian nuclear weapon, Riyadh might be willing to forgo these subsidies and accept the risk of domestic dissent if it believed that the oil weapon stood a chance at halting the nuclear program or altering the regime's behavior.

The diverse views of the other Gulf states present leverage and risks for the United States. As noted earlier, observers frequently assume that the smaller states of the Gulf will coalesce behind Saudi

---

[16] Stewart, 2010a.

[17] With respect to Chinese direct investment in Iran's energy sector, Iran actually enjoys some advantage over Saudi Arabia in terms of its more permissive regulatory environment. Specifically, whereas Saudi Arabia still restricts foreign investment in its upstream oil sector (exploration and production), Iran has a mechanism that allows China to develop Iranian fields in return for a share of that field's future production. See Wehrey, Kaye, et al., 2010, pp. 55–61.

[18] Hannah, 2009.

Arabia on Iran policy, given Riyadh's weight in the GCC and its privileged relationship with the United States. Yet this thinking ignores the distinctiveness of the Gulf states' respective bilateral relations with the Islamic Republic and the impact that their domestic politics have on their foreign policy.[19]

Kuwait and Bahrain have historically lined up with the alarmist Saudi position, but both states are constrained in their maneuverability because of their fractious domestic politics and sectarian makeup. In Kuwait, there are recent signs that the country's relations with Iran might be thawing, particularly in the area of trade, under the leadership of Prime Minister Nasser Al-Mohammed al-Sabah (Kuwait's former ambassador to Iran)—a reorientation that has threatened to bring down the government in the face of concerted opposition by a Sunni-dominated parliament.[20] Parliamentary opposition by Shi'a deputies also limited Kuwait's contribution of forces to the deployment of the Saudi-led Peninsula Shield force into Bahrain.[21] For its part, Bahrain's traditionally helpful role as the seat of the U.S. Fifth Fleet has been shaken by fierce protest, and the resulting crackdown has severely tarnished the al-Khalifa ruling family's legitimacy.

The remaining GCC states—Qatar, Oman, and the United Arab Emirates (UAE)—have more-varied perspectives on Iran, with important implications for U.S. strategy. For the United States, Qatar presents both assets and liabilities. Its regional mediation efforts with Tehran, hosting of U.S. forces, soft-power capability embodied in *al-Jazeera*, and confidence-building measures are mostly helpful, but its opportunistic outreach to Iran could also be worrisome, depending on the nature of U.S. strategy. Perhaps more than any other Gulf state, Qatar has exploited tensions with Iran to carve out a highly independent, proactive, and, at times, paradoxical foreign policy. Many of its policies toward Iran appear designed to subvert the influence of its historical Arab foe, Saudi Arabia, by rallying a competing Arab consensus. Qatar has also worked with Tehran on mediating disputes outside

---

[19] Alshayji, 2002.

[20] Hasan, 2011.

[21] "MPs, Media Hype Hiking Sectarian Tension Locally," 2011.

the Gulf, particularly in Lebanon, while making vocal acknowledgments of Iran's status as a "neighbor" and not an "enemy."[22] But the relationship is not without tension: Doha has found itself explicitly threatened with Iranian retaliation because of the U.S. military presence on its soil.[23]

Oman's close ties with Tehran enable it to act as an intermediary and emissary—a role illustrated most recently by Sultan Qaboos's success in gaining the release of U.S. hikers held captive by Tehran.[24] Similarly to Qatar, Oman has long enjoyed warm relations with Iran, stemming from its proximity and shared sense of culture, history, and trade.[25] On the Iranian nuclear issue, Oman has evinced a posture of quiet concern and even resignation, with senior officials telling RAND researchers that they had greater worries about a nuclear Pakistan and that Oman could ultimately live with a nuclear Iran. Like Qatar, Oman has resisted Saudi efforts to build Gulf consensus against Iran, partly due to its long-standing territorial disputes with the kingdom.

The UAE occupies a unique position as a U.S. partner, bulwark, and neutral meeting ground. Among the major sources of tension with Iran is the territorial dispute over Abu Musa and the Greater and Lesser Tunbs islands, although this is more a concern for Abu Dhabi than for the other four emirates. Dubai's relations with Iran have traditionally been the warmest, given the influence of Iranian investment and its large Iranian expatriate population, numbering nearly half a million. Given these divisions, the UAE's posture as a whole toward Iran has long straddled a balance between hostility and accommodation. From Washington's perspective, both Dubai and Abu Dhabi have taken proactive steps to enforce sanctions against Iranian banks and individuals

---

[22] Qatar's stance is also shaped by its shared control with Iran of the North Field/South Pars offshore natural-gas field.

[23] Guitta, 2007.

[24] "Clinton," 2010.

[25] Between 1970 and 1977, Oman received substantial Iranian military assistance from the shah in fighting an insurgency in Oman's underdeveloped province of Dhofar; memory of this aid continues to inform Oman's favorable views of Iran. For background on Oman's posture toward Saudi Arabia and Iran, see Kechichian, 1995, pp. 66–76.

affiliated with the Revolutionary Guards.[26] Much of this activity stems from Dubai's credit crisis and resulting dependence on assistance from Abu Dhabi, which has produced greater unanimity in the UAE's Iran policy.[27]

Key Areas of U.S. Leverage

By virtue of their geographic position, energy resources, and history of interaction with Iran, Saudi Arabia and the GCC comprise a contested arena in the U.S.-Iranian relationship. Indeed, many of the fundamental problems in this relationship concern regional views regarding Iran's proper place in the Gulf system. Is Iran a coequal neighbor in the Gulf, a "first among equals," or a regional hegemon? From the GCC—and especially Saudi—perspective, any acceptance of Iran into the Gulf system would entail a de facto recognition of Iranian dominance, given the Arab GCC's demographic, economic, and military inferiority. Despite this perception of threat, GCC responses to U.S. policies toward Iran are more measured and nuanced than commonly assumed, offering both leverage and liabilities for key U.S. policy objectives.

- *Halting Iran's nuclear capabilities.* On the effort to halt the Iranian nuclear program, the Gulf Arab states can assist the United States in the enforcement of sanctions but should not be expected to vocally condemn Iran's nuclear ambitions, given the public sensitivities outlined above. Saudi diplomacy and economic resources can be similarly useful in building regional consensus on the nuclear program, but Riyadh is unlikely to use price quotas in OPEC (i.e., the oil weapon) as leverage on the nuclear issue.
- *Containing Iran's regional influence.* With regard to Iran's regional influence, the past several years have shown the value and risks of Saudi efforts to contain and roll back Iranian activities in Leb-

---

[26] RAND meetings with officials in Abu Dhabi and Dubai, May 2010.

[27] Worth, Timmons, and Thomas, 2009.

anon, Gaza, and, to a lesser extent, Iraq. In some cases, Saudi
efforts to build consensus against Iran have been deliberately
thwarted by Qatar. Moreover, at the level of public discourse,
the Gulf states continue to maintain that movement on Arab-
Israeli peace is a critical element of undermining Iran's malignant
activities and rejectionist appeal. "Solve the Palestinian issue," one
Kuwaiti diplomat noted in a 2006 interview, "and you'll defang
Iran."[28] Saudi-sponsored peace initiatives are helpful in this regard
but face the same stumbling blocks as United States–sponsored
efforts. Gulf Arab officials have also become increasingly alarmed
about Iran's ability to exploit the unrest and disarray of the recent
Arab revolts. Yet, in some cases, particularly in Saudi Arabia, this
vocal concern about Iran might be an attempt to shift the focus
away from what those officials perceive as the more proximate and
pressing threat: popular dissent against Arab authoritarian rule.
This is especially true with regard to Bahrain, where the al-Khalifa
ruling family and its Saudi patrons have made numerous charges
about Iran's role in inciting and sustaining the Shi'a-dominated
protests, with little evidence. In the case of Bahrain and other
fractured states in the region, the most expeditious way to blunt
Iranian influence might be genuine political reform that bolsters
popular perceptions of regime legitimacy and mitigates the long-
standing public grievances (particularly among the Shi'a) that
Tehran has sought to exploit. For obvious reasons, Gulf regimes
might find this policy less attractive than the more traditional
containment approach that relies on diplomatic and military support from the United States. Yet concern about their domestic
opinion, which is, in general, less anti-Iranian than official views
are, limits how far they will go in associating themselves with
such U.S. efforts.

- *Influencing Iran's political evolution.* On the issue of political
  change in Iran, the Gulf states have limited resources and willingness. As noted, from the Gulf Arab perspective, the possibility
  of a reformist or pragmatist government in Iran might change

---

[28] Author's interview with Kuwaiti diplomat, Kuwait City, February 2006.

the *tone* of Iranian policy in the Gulf but would not substantially alter Iran's historical drive for regional primacy. And Gulf regimes are similarly concerned that a warming of U.S.-Iranian relations would supplant their own privileged relationship with the United States and that liberalization in Iran would inspire similar demands for change among their own publics.

- *U.S. leverage and influence in the Gulf.* Arms sales can be a useful instrument of U.S. leverage over the GCC, even if their actual security benefit to these states is negligible in the short term (given the time required to develop proficiency and interoperability).[29] The sales might have the added benefit of raising the stature of Saudi Arabia in the inter-Arab arena, thus aiding Saudi diplomatic initiatives to counter Iranian influence in the Levant, as well as in the Gulf. But, as noted, arms transfers do little to address the more-menacing aspects of Iran's ideological challenge. Here, the United States should continue to push for measured reform and liberalization in the Gulf, to bolster the domestic legitimacy of Gulf regimes and to make them more confident of their publics' loyalty and support (and thus decrease the fissures that Iran can exploit). Finally, the Gulf Security Dialogue is an important means of U.S. influence over the smaller Gulf states; by engaging these states on security issues at the bilateral level, the United States raises their stature within the GCC and is thus more likely to solicit their individual cooperation on Iran—whether as intermediaries or as partners in enforcing sanctions. Conversely, expectations that the GCC should act as a united "bloc" against Iran are likely to fall short, given the diversity of views of the member states.

---

[29] For more on the GCC as an effectively hollow military force, see Cordesman and Nerguizian, 2010. They write that the GCC's "lack of cooperation, interoperability, and serious exercise activity cripples their ability to act with any unity and makes them more of a facade than a force. It also makes them far more dependent on the US, while limiting their collective ability to fight alongside the US in a major crisis."

Israel

The Israeli government has no real influence in Tehran but has a lot in Washington. Concern over Israel's security is not the only motivation for U.S. policy toward Iran, but it is one of the most important. It is what principally distinguishes the level of U.S. concern over Iranian nuclear proliferation from the much more-advanced efforts of Pakistan, India, or North Korea.

Halting Iran's Nuclear Capabilities

Israel views Iran's pursuit of nuclear capabilities with great alarm. Israeli officials believe that Iran's intent is to weaponize its nuclear enrichment capabilities, and they view this threat to be Israel's greatest security challenge.[30] Israel's concerns over Iran's nuclear drive are often expressed in existential terms, even if there is some debate within the security establishment about using such a dire term.[31] Israelis across the political spectrum believe that actual Iranian use of nuclear weapons against Israel is a real possibility, particularly given the widespread view that extremist ideology is a major driver of Iranian actions.[32] Such views are more prevalent among the political elite than among intelligence and security analysts, who tend to see Iranian nuclear pursuits as more closely tied to ambitions for regional influence than to aims to destroy Israel. Likewise, prominent Israeli experts on deterrence ques-

---

[30] Author discussions with dozens of Israeli officials and analysts in Tel Aviv and Jerusalem, August 2010.

[31] Defense Minister Ehud Barak has stopped using the term *existential*, arguing that this rhetoric makes Israel look weak and undermines Israeli deterrence. Those holding this view also believe that speaking in existential terms makes the Iran problem about Israel rather than an international challenge. Other leaders, such as national security adviser Uzi Arad and Mossad head Meir Dagan, still use this terminology, believing that such alarmist rhetoric is necessary in order to "scare the world" into action (discussion with Israeli expert on Iran, Los Angeles, October 2010).

[32] Although reference to the Holocaust has been "rarely invoked, except on the extremes, in Israeli politics," "the Iranian threat has returned the Final Solution to the heart of Israeli discourse," according to Yossi Klein Halevi and Michael B. Oren (now Israeli ambassador to the United States). Also see Freilich, 2010.

tion the probability of intentional Iranian nuclear use against Israel, given the latter's considerable deterrent capabilities.[33]

But political leaders, and even some Iran analysts within Israel's strategic community both inside and outside the government, take Iran's ideological hostility toward Israel and the prospect of it leading to nuclear use seriously. As one analyst explained, "If I were the Prime Minister, could I afford to risk this assumption [that Iran can be deterred] being wrong?"[34] Israelis also worry that, even if Iran would not intentionally use nuclear weapons against Israel, the potential for unintended use, accidents, and escalation would pose a significant risk, given the short distances in the region and the absence of either normal diplomatic or crisis "hotline" links between Israel and Iran.[35]

Perhaps even more than they have fear of an Iranian bomb being used against them, Israelis worry about other spillover effects of a bomb and are particularly concerned that an Iranian nuclear cover will make allies, such as Hizballah, more aggressive while limiting Israel's own ability to retaliate. Israeli officials and analysts also believe an Iranian nuclear bomb will fundamentally alter the regional balance of power, undermining U.S. influence and moving Iran's neighbors further into its orbit. At the same time, there is a widespread assumption among Israeli strategic analysts that a nuclear-armed Iran will lead other states, including Saudi Arabia, Egypt, and Turkey, to follow suit, leading to a destabilizing, multipolar, nuclear regional security environment.[36]

---

[33] Evron, 2008, p. 52.

[34] Israeli security analyst, Tel Aviv, August 16, 2010.

[35] Prominent Israeli experts on deterrence question the probability of intentional Iranian nuclear use against Israel because,

> in view of Israel's widely assumed large nuclear arsenal and numerous delivery vehicles . . . it appears highly improbable that even a fanatic leadership would choose such a policy. . . . No regime, even if endowed with the most extreme ideology, chooses to commit suicide. (Evron, 2008, p. 52)

Similar concerns were expressed in interviews with the author in meetings in Israel with officials and analysts, Tel Aviv and Jerusalem, August 2010.

[36] For further examination of the reasons Israel is concerned about Iran's nuclear program, see E. Sadr, 2005.

Constraining Iran's Regional Influence

Israel is concerned about Iran's growing regional influence and reach in the past decade, particularly the extension of its influence to Israel's borders in Lebanon and Gaza.[37] Many officials and security analysts believe that Iran is seeking not only regional dominance but also global influence, challenging the status quo as a revolutionary, radical power.[38] In response to a visit by President Ahmadinejad to southern Lebanon, Israeli minister Uzi Landau suggested, "The lesson we should learn from Ahmadinejad's visit is that Iran is on the northern border of Israel."[39] Israeli officials and many nongovernmental analysts also believe that Iran's hegemonic ambitions are driven not only by its strategic interest in challenging Israel as its main competitor for regional dominance but also by an ideological purpose to destroy the Jewish state itself.[40] Although Iran's ideological framing of its anti-Israel rhetoric might be masking underlying geopolitical motives, Israelis nonetheless take this ideology seriously. The fall of pro-Western leaders in Egypt and Tunisia and widespread regional unrest have only enhanced Israeli concerns about Iran and Iran's ability to capitalize on the regional turmoil, leading to what Foreign Minister Avigdor Lieberman called the "Iranization of the region."[41]

Influencing Iran's Internal Political Evolution

The perceived ideological nature of the Iranian regime, combined with the consolidation of the principlists' power within the government

---

[37] For a more detailed discussion of rising Iranian influence, particularly in the aftermath of the 2003 Iraq war, see Wehrey, Kaye, et al., 2010.

[38] Interviews with Israeli officials and analysts, Tel Aviv and Jerusalem, August 2010.

[39] Quoted in Worth, 2010b.

[40] A Foreign Ministry assessment argues,

> The total delegitimization of Israel's existence, which lies at the heart of Iran's policy, is based on deep ideological foundations and attracts growing popular support not only among Shi'ites but also among Sunnis. Alongside the United States ("the great Satan"), Israel ("the little Satan") is the primary focus for incitement and subversion. . . . (Etzion, 2009, p. 53)

[41] See Keinon, 2011, p. 2.

since the 2009 presidential election, heightens Israeli threat perceptions of Iran's nuclear program and regional ambitions. Some Israeli analysts point out that Israel does not raise objections to a Pakistani nuclear bomb because that nation, even though Islamic, is not threatening to "wipe Israel off the map" or supporting organizations engaged in killing Israeli civilians.[42] The implication, of course, is that a different type of Iranian leadership would fundamentally shift Israeli threat perceptions of Iran and its nuclear program.

However, Israelis do not hold much hope for the Green Movement succeeding, and they recognize that even reformist opposition leaders would have motivations to pursue a nuclear capability. The Israelis would prefer fundamental regime change that leads to the demise of the Islamic Republic and a return to a secular (if, perhaps, conservative and authoritarian) regime. Many Israelis still have positive memories of close relations with Iran under the shah.[43] Yet some Israeli analysts warn of the dangers of assuming that a return to a periphery doctrine (cooperation with non-Arab allies) is possible in today's geostrategic environment, in which Iran might pose a strategic challenge to Israel under any form of government.[44] Still, Israelis would welcome any challenge to the current regime, so, not surprisingly, many Israeli officials expressed some disappointment that the Obama administration did not react more forcefully in support of the Green Movement following the 2009 presidential election and subsequent repression in Iran.[45] But it is not clear that any Israeli policies can constructively affect internal dynamics within Iran, except to avoid a military strike that might arguably consolidate the regime's power and increase the repression of the opposition.

Israel is wary of U.S. engagement with Iran, fearing that any accommodation policies toward Iran will come at Israel's expense. An Israeli expert on Iran suggested that support for U.S. engagement of

---

[42] Interviews with Israeli officials and analysts, Tel Aviv and Jerusalem, October 2010.

[43] For further details of this relationship, which, in reality, was often strained, see Parsi, 2007.

[44] Interview with security analyst, Tel Aviv, October 2010.

[45] Interviews with Israeli officials, Jerusalem, October 2010.

Iran increased for a time only because it was viewed as a necessary step for the United States to show that it had taken all measures possible so as to facilitate tougher actions in the future (including a military option). However, Israelis presumed that engagement would fail, preferring stronger economic pressure, particularly on Iran's energy sector, backed by the threat of military action.[46] Under Obama, the United States has ratcheted up international sanctions while making several diplomatic overtures and remaining largely silent on the "military option." Indeed, U.S. officials have repeatedly expressed caution about the utility of a preventive strike on Iran's nuclear facilities. President George W. Bush is said to have discouraged the Israelis from attacking Iran at the end of his administration, and this policy stance has presumably continued into the Obama administration, even as U.S. officials have talked down the prospect of a U.S. strike without renouncing the possibility altogether.[47]

In contrast, although Israeli officials rarely speak in detail about a military strike, they frequently repeat the mantra that "all options are on the table."[48] A report by a well-known Israeli journalist suggests that, in quiet deliberations, senior Israeli officials are seriously considering this option and believe that Iranian retaliation would likely be limited.[49] Benjamin Netanyahu's national security adviser, Uzi Arad, has stated publicly that he believes that the international community would back an Israeli military strike: "I don't see anyone who questions

---

[46] Israeli expert on Iran, Los Angeles, September 30, 2010. An Israeli official similarly suggested in an interview that she favored President Obama's initial engagement efforts because they forced the United States "to learn the hard way that engagement will not work" and why this Iranian regime is not serious (interview with Israeli official, Tel Aviv, August 16, 2010).

[47] Klein, 2010.

[48] According to Ehud Yaari, "The military and intelligence communities are under strict instructions to avoid making remarks except to affirm that Israel is preparing itself for 'any eventuality.'" Yaari also notes that there is little public discussion in Israel about its options toward Iran (Yaari, 2009).

[49] According to this report, senior Israeli officials argue that Iranian retaliation through Hizballah or HAMAS might be constrained because both groups would want to avoid retaliation in Lebanon and Gaza. See Yaari, 2009. Author interviews with Israeli officials and analysts in Tel Aviv and Jerusalem in August 2010 revealed similar thinking.

the legality of this or the legitimacy. . . . They only discuss the efficacy, which is interesting. It suggests that people understand the problem."[50] Other Israeli leaders arguing for a military option suggest that the negative consequences of an Israeli attack might be exaggerated or that the risks of an attack might outweigh the costs of doing nothing.[51] According to this view, Israel might have to attack Iran even if the United States opposes the action. As one former official asked, "do you think Netanyahu is going to tell his grandchildren that he didn't stop the Iranian bomb because of pressure from Clinton?"[52]

But other assessments also recognize that a unilateral Israeli attack, although possible, would be complicated due to overflight requirements and long distances, among other operational and political risks.[53] Israeli leaders are aware that a military strike on Iran would be far more difficult and complicated than previous attacks on Iraq and Syria's nuclear sites and would likely only delay but not destroy the program.[54] As a retired Israeli general put it, "If there's no choice, Israel can set back the Iranian nuclear process" but would be unable to launch a sustained campaign to stop it and would likely face Iranian retaliation through ballistic-missile attacks directed against Israel.[55] Although such cautious assessments of a military option have existed for some time, public statements in 2011 by the outgoing head of the Mossad, Meir Dagan, suggesting that a military strike would

---

[50] Quoted in Zacharia, 2010. Similar views were expressed in author interviews in Jerusalem and Tel Aviv with Israeli officials, August 2010. Some officials argued that, to avoid bringing the United States into the conflict, Iran would not retaliate against the United States. Others suggested that any amount of retaliation would be worth the costs if the alternative were a nuclear-armed Iran.

[51] Such sentiment was conveyed by a senior Israeli official at a conference attended by one of the authors, Washington, D.C., January 2010.

[52] Interview with former Israeli official, Herzliya, August 2010.

[53] For a detailed assessment of an Israeli military strike on Iran, see Allin and Simon, 2010, and Toukan and Cordesman, 2009. For further details on a potential Israeli military attack and an argument emphasizing its dangers, see Rogers, 2010.

[54] See, for example, "Israelis Ponder the Perils of Hitting Iran," 2009.

[55] "Israelis Ponder the Perils of Hitting Iran," 2009.

be "stupid" brought these internal Israeli debates out into the open.[56] But, despite these differences in cost-benefit assessments among Israeli leaders, there is a near consensus in Israeli strategic circles that, even if Israel could effectively attack Iran, it is preferable that the United States take action. Thus, the United States can expect continued pressure from across the political spectrum in Israel—as well as from Israel's supporters in the United States—to actively keep the U.S. military option open.

Israeli timelines are also shorter, with assessments of Iran's nuclear progress often more dire than U.S. assessments, even if, in recent months, the Israelis have expressed less alarmist estimates of the Iranian nuclear timeline. The 2007 U.S. National Intelligence Estimate (NIE)—suggesting that Iran had halted its nuclear weapon developments—was particularly alarming to Israelis, leading to sharp and negative responses. Israeli officials have recently proclaimed timelines that seem more closely aligned with those assessed by the United States because they believe that economic pressure and alleged sabotage tactics against Iran are having some effect. For example, former Mossad head Meir Dagan stated in early January 2011 that Iran would not be able to produce a nuclear weapon until 2015, and Israel's deputy prime minister, Moshe Ya'alon, suggested that the West had up to three years to prevent Iran from acquiring a nuclear weapon.[57]

Finally, the United States and Israel have different priorities. The United States is currently engaged in wars in Iraq and Afghanistan and focused on countering the threat emanating from al Qaeda. Iran plays both a destabilizing and stabilizing role in both countries yet has, on occasion, also cooperated with the United States because of common threats (e.g., the Taliban and al Qaeda). Although the United States considers the extremism emanating from Iraq and Afghanistan to be a direct challenge to U.S. interests, it views the Iranian nuclear program as a broader international challenge. The United States is actively attempting to prevent Iranian nuclear weaponization and to assure U.S. partners in the face of this challenge with stepped-up secu-

[56] See Melman, 2011.

[57] See Solomon and Levinson, 2011, and Ignatius, 2011.

rity cooperation and arms sales, but the nuclear challenge nonetheless competes with other demands on the United States as a global power. In contrast, the Iranian nuclear issue has, until very recently, been the top priority for Israeli policymakers, and Israelis fear that, because the United States is distracted with other pressing challenges at home and abroad, it might have already accepted a nuclear Iran.[58] Because of this anxiety, Secretary of State Hillary Clinton's notion of providing a U.S. "nuclear" or "defense umbrella" for regional allies backfired in Israel: Israelis interpreted this statement as a shift from a policy of preemption to one of deterrence of a nuclear-armed Iran, as, indeed, it would seem to be.[59]

In recent years, the large military aid packages to Israel have been supplemented with additional security cooperation and equipment (particularly in the missile defense area) to bolster Israeli confidence and security in the face of growing anxiety about Iranian influence. Toward the end of the George W. Bush administration, for example, the United States delivered the X-band radar system, a sophisticated, long-range early-warning radar that can detect targets from thousands of miles away, making it a particularly important system for future contingencies involving Iran.[60] U.S.-Israeli joint exercises have also focused on missile defense, testing multiple missile defense systems to improve interoperability.[61] Israeli news reports discuss such exercises in the context of countering accelerated Iranian ballistic-missile development and defending Israel against future attacks.[62] The Obama administration also recently announced the sale of the advanced F-35 joint

---

[58] This sentiment was expressed in several meetings with Israeli officials and analysts in Jerusalem and Tel Aviv, August 2010.

[59] As one senior Israeli security source is quoted as saying, "What is the significance of such guarantee when it comes from those who hesitated to deal with a non-nuclear Iran? What kind of credibility would this [guarantee have] when Iran is nuclear-capable?" (quoted in Benn and Haaretz correspondent, 2008). Also see Guzansky, 2009, p. 88.

[60] The delivery took place on September 21, 2008. See Putrich, 2008.

[61] See Prusher, 2009.

[62] See Katz, 2009a, 2009b, and 2009c.

strike fighters to Israel.[63] In addition to enhanced security cooperation, the United States continues to be Israel's closest political ally at the UN, and President Obama has reaffirmed the U.S. commitment to support Israel's policy of nuclear ambiguity despite his administration's active nonproliferation agenda.

This extensive support has not always been reciprocated by the Israelis on issues of importance to Washington. Israeli settlement in the West Bank and East Jerusalem has continued despite U.S. objections. Turkey has produced more success in easing the Israeli blockade of Gaza than did the United States. Rocket attacks following the Lebanon and then Gaza withdrawals, as well as the flotilla incident with Turkey, have reinforced a siege mentality in Israel. Many there believe that Israel will be blamed no matter what it does, leading to more-defiant positions. The Egyptian revolution and the interim military regime's opening of the Gaza crossing and promotion of Fatah-HAMAS reconciliation has heightened this sense of isolation. The result so far has been to intensify both Israel's cooperation with the United States and its resistance to U.S. efforts to broker peace with its Palestinian neighbors.

Although the Israeli and U.S. governments both recognize a connection between the Iranian threat and the occupation of the West Bank and Gaza, they come to diametrically opposite policy conclusions. Washington believes that a settlement with the Palestinians would dramatically undercut Iran's influence in the Arab world. The Israeli government maintains that such a settlement is impossible as long as Iran backs rejectionist elements among the Palestinians and other Arab societies.

Turkey

Turkey does not want a nuclear-armed Iran, but neither does it fear Iran as a military threat.[64] Turkish cooperation with Iran has increased

---

[63] "Israel Wants More Stealth Fighters," 2010.

[64] Yetkin, 2010. We thank Mustafa Oguz for research assistance on this section.

under the Justice and Development Party (Adalet ve Kalkınma Partisi, or AKP) leadership since 2002, leading to the formulation of less hostile threat assessments in official Turkish security doctrine.[65] Turkey regularly defends Iran's right to acquire nuclear technology and does not believe that economic sanctions are an effective tool to halt Iran's nuclear program, preferring diplomatic solutions.[66] Turkey is also concerned about a possible U.S. military attack on Iran and, to avoid such action, tries to defuse tension over Iran's nuclear program.[67]

Beyond the nuclear issue, Turkey shares some interests with Iran, such as opposition to Kurdish separatism and support for the territorial integrity of Iraq. To this end, Iran joined the Iraq Neighbors Group set up by Turkey in 2003.[68] The AKP's Islamic identity arguably also enhances its affinity with Iran, despite the Sunni-Shi'a divide.[69] Turkey has developed extensive trade relations with Tehran and is interested in further investment in Iran's energy sector. Turkish-Iranian trade rose from $1 billion to $10 billion from 2002 to 2011, and one-fifth of Turkish natural gas is provided by Iran (which is Turkey's second-largest supplier, after Russia).[70]

On the other hand, Turkey views Iran as a political rival in Iraq and actively works with Sunni groups to counter Shi'a influence.[71] Turkey is also concerned about growing Iranian influence in the Israeli-Palestinian arena and has thus sought to challenge Iran by develop-

---

[65] Iran's nuclear and missile program topped the list in Turkey's 2005 Red Book (officially known as the National Security Policy Document), which outlines security threats against the country. According to Aydıntaşbaş Asli Aydıntaşbaş, "The expectation is that the new document will reflect a new period of cooperation with Iran, Baghdad and Barzani, along with a revision of regional alliances" ("Kırmızı Kitap'ta Köklü Değişim," 2010).

[66] See Fairclough and Blumenstein, 2010.

[67] Taşpınar, 2010a.

[68] Kramer, 2010, p. 15.

[69] A former Turkish foreign minister and retired ambassador, İlter Türkmen, stated, for example, that the AKP romanticizes Islam, leading to a strong Islamic solidarity with like-minded actors (Düzel, 2010).

[70] D-8 Organization for Economic Cooperation, 2010.

[71] Taşpınar, 2010b.

ing closer ties to both HAMAS and, until recently, Syria, becoming increasingly vocal in this area since Israel's Operation Cast Lead in Gaza. In its challenge to Iran, Turkey has been critical of the conservative leadership in Jordan and the Palestinian Authority (PA), boosting its own appeal among neighboring Muslim populations with its recognition of HAMAS as the "legitimate government of the Palestinian people" and challenging Israeli policies, such as through the 2010 flotilla incident.[72]

Turkish views and policies toward Iran are a mix of cooperation and rivalry. Like the United States, Turkey is concerned about Iran's growing regional influence. However, Turkey believes that the best way to counter that influence is by reaching out to Iran's allies (e.g., Syria, Hizballah, and HAMAS) in an attempt to moderate their behavior and limit their dependency on Iran. For example, AKP officials have appealed to HAMAS to act like a political party instead of like a violent organization, and they lobbied HAMAS to release the kidnapped Israeli soldier (Gilad Shalit) even after the flotilla incident.[73] AKP officials also took credit for the cease-fire between HAMAS and Fatah, alienating Egyptian officials, although some analysts argue that the AKP might exaggerate Turkish influence over these actors.[74] Some Israeli sources claim that the Turkish government supports Hizballah, but the Turkish Foreign Ministry has denied such claims.[75] Another Israeli source reported that Turkey actually stopped a Hizballah attack

---

[72] See Çağaptay, 2010.

[73] "Turkish Foreign Policy," 2010.

[74] Senior foreign policy columnist Semih İdiz argues that Turkey's influence on HAMAS is exaggerated by Turkish officials. See İdiz, 2010. Also see an International Crisis Group interview with an Arab diplomat in Turkey and the Middle East, International Crisis Group, 2010a, p. 18.

[75] One source claiming that there is Turkish support for Hizballah is "Iran to Give Hizbullah Weapons," 2010.

According to a Turkish news report,

> Turkey's new spy chief [Hakan] Fidan is a source of concern for Israel whose defense minister earlier expressed the concern that Ankara could pass secret information to Israel's arch-foe Iran, because its new intelligence chief supported the Islamic Republic. Turkey communicated its dissatisfaction with the Israeli government by summoning

on an Israeli target inside Turkey that aimed to avenge Hizballah leader Mughniyeh's death.[76]

The Turkish government's view regarding the Iran-aligned group reflects the voter base of the ruling AKP party, which considers Hizballah and HAMAS to be legitimate resistance organizations against Israel and sympathizes with Iran because of its stance against the United States. Such popular sentiment poses a barrier to more-cooperative Turkish policies related to other U.S. goals vis-à-vis Iran.

Ankara believes that sanctions will undermine Turkish business interests, will strengthen Iran's hard-line regime, and are unlikely to work.[77] Turkey voted against the UN Security Council sanction resolution in June 2010 (although it has agreed to abide by the resolution) and did not support subsequent, follow-on sanctions imposed by the United States, Europe, and other allies.[78]

Prime Minister Erdoğan has publicly supported Iran's right to develop a peaceful nuclear program and has dismissed claims of Iranian nuclear weapon ambitions as "mere gossip," even if AKP officials might privately acknowledge that they believe Iran is seeking a weapon capability.[79] Still, Turkish officials argue that all states in the region (including Israel) should give up nuclear weapons and establish a nuclear weapon–free zone and that pressuring Iran without equal pressure on Israel suggests Western double standards. The Turkish military might be more concerned about Iran's nuclear development than about the ruling AKP, but its role in Turkish politics has been diminishing.[80]

---

the ambassador to the Foreign Ministry in Ankara to protest against Barak's remarks. ("Turkish Foreign Ministry Denies Hezbollah Arms Claims as Baseless," 2010)

[76] Issacharoff, 2009.

[77] Nahmias, 2010.

[78] MacFarquhar, 2010.

[79] International Crisis Group, 2010b, p. 12. In an interview published in *Forbes*, Turkish President Gül stated that Iran is after the bomb, but a later declaration by the president's office denied that Gül ever gave such an interview.

[80] Many retired and senior military officials were jailed recently on the grounds of being members of an alleged terrorist organization that aimed to topple the government with a coup d'état. Although the military is not taking public positions on the Iranian nuclear file

AKP officials oppose a U.S. or Israeli military strike, believing that a preemptive attack on Iranian nuclear installations would, at best, only delay Iran's program and reinforce the regime's resolve to acquire a weapon capability.[81] Turkey has sealed its air space to Israeli military aircraft.[82] Such an Israeli or U.S. attack would likely generate considerable sympathy toward Iran among both the Turkish public and government, further straining relations with Israel and Washington.

Rather than additional sanctions or a military option, the Turkish government favors engagement with Iran, and Turkish public opinion supports this stance.[83] The United States has not always welcomed Turkish diplomatic efforts to resolve the nuclear issue, as evidenced by the U.S. rejection of the Turkish and Brazilian nuclear swap deal negotiated with Iran in May 2010. This failed deal proved a serious blow to U.S.-Turkish relations, given the Turkish perception that it was delivering a compromise the U.S. administration had backed.[84]

With respect to Iran's internal developments, Turkey is careful not to intervene in the domestic affairs of its neighbor, viewing the destabilization of the Iranian regime as a security risk. As Turkish officials put it, "We don't want a nuclear Iran, Iran destabilizing the region or a de-stable [sic] Iran."[85] The AKP government was among the first to congratulate Ahmadinejad on his election victory in June 2009. Turkish President Abdullah Gül and Prime Minister Tayyip Erdoğan called Ahmadinejad to congratulate him even before the Iranian Elec-

---

given this domestic turmoil, the 2005 Red Book and its emphasis on Iran's missile program as a regional threat suggest that the military might be more concerned about Iranian nuclear developments than the ruling AKP. In contrast, Prime Minister Erdoğan believes that, for decades, Turkey wasted its resources on "virtual enemies" and that Greece's economic crisis is caused by high defense spending. As he explains, "The cost of manufacturing virtual enemies is very high in our neighbor. We must avoid the same mistake" ("Erdoğan," 2010).

[81] See "Turkish President Voices Concern over Military Action on Iran," 2010.

[82] "İsrail yeni hava sahası bakıyor," 2010.

[83] German Marshall Fund of the United States, 2010.

[84] For a detailed discussion of the nuclear deal and misperceptions on both the Turkish and U.S. sides, see International Crisis Group, 2010b, pp. 12–14.

[85] International Crisis Group, 2010b, p. 12.

tion Board announced official results, leading some Turkish analysts to question the ruling party's unequivocal support for an undemocratic and repressive regime.[86]

With its firm victory in the constitutional-amendment referendum, lack of a powerful opposition, and a renewed mandate in 2011, there does not seem to be a rival to the ruling AKP party in the near future. The AKP might believe that the United States needs Turkey more than Turkey needs the United States, particularly because it is not pursuing European Union (EU) membership (which the United States supports) as actively as past governments have. Yet, despite the AKP's tendency to capitalize on anti–United States and anti-Israeli public sentiment, Turkey maintains important tools to help advance U.S. policy toward Iran, particularly through its diplomacy and by offering an alternative model both to Iran and to the authoritarian Arab regimes.

The Turkish government has access to the highest levels of the Iranian regime, potentially providing a helpful conduit for U.S. positions, provided that U.S.-Turkish communication is clear. But it is the Turkish social model that might prove the most crucial instrument to contribute to U.S. policy vis-à-vis Iran. As a Jordanian commentator observes, "unlike the Iranian model, the Turkish model that is based on 'soft power' enjoys international credibility and respect."[87] Turkish international relations professor Beril Dedeoğlu suggests that Turkey's involvement in the Palestinian issue undercuts Iranian influence there: "Turkey's engagement with Hamas will definitely help Hamas free itself of Iranian influence. . . ."[88] A U.S.-based Turkey analyst similarly argues,

---

[86] After Iran's crackdown on protesters, Soli Özel wrote, "Preservation of the Iranian regime's democratic dimension should be something that Turkey cares about. On the contrary, despite all blatant cheating, the Turkish Prime Minister argued that elections were fair and legitimate" (Özel, 2010).

[87] Al-Rintawi, 2010.

[88] Zeynalov, 2010.

Iran and Hizballah have been able to win the hearts and minds of the Arab street in Cairo, Amman, Damascus, etc. In that sense, a clear strategic goal of Turkey is to contain Tehran's influence. Turkey is doing so by successfully cultivating Damascus and slowly co-opting Hamas. Turkey's recent spat with Israel has also transformed Recep Tayyip Erdoğan into a hero in the eyes of the Arab street at the expense of Hassan Nasrallah and Ahmadinejad. Trying to strengthen moderate elements in Tehran that want dialogue with Washington is also part of the Turkish strategy. Sadly, this Turkish policy of containing radical influences in Iran is not well understood in Washington.[89]

Turkey is unlikely to warm to U.S. pressure tactics on Iran, and the ruling party finds political value in touting its independence from U.S. policies.[90] U.S. policymakers should thus recognize the limits of just how far Turkey will be willing to go in aligning its positions with U.S. Iran policy. However, U.S. policy could capitalize on the Turkish desire to stem Iranian regional influence, particularly through Turkey's soft-power outreach to a range of regional actors, even if many of those actors are U.S. adversaries. If Turkish soft-power appeal succeeds to any extent in limiting Iran's regional influence, that is a net gain for U.S. Iran policy.

Syria

With the current turmoil and crackdown in Syria following waves of popular protests beginning in March 2011, Syria's ability to take actions that could help facilitate a U.S. Iran strategy is questionable. Yet the fall of the Assad regime would represent a severe blow to Iranian capacity to project regional influence.

---

[89] Taşpınar, 2010b.

[90] "'We are no more a country that is directed from a center. We are not piece of cake' said Turkish Foreign Minister Davutoğlu when explaining divergence of Turkey with the US on Iran's nuclear program" ("Türkiye artık çantada keklik değil," 2010).

The Assad regime is likely to remain internally focused for some time, assuming that it manages to stay in power. And the regime's brutal repression of the opposition has frozen any attempts by the United States or the EU to draw Syria away from Iran's orbit through economic and political inducements (such a "peeling" strategy was often discussed before this dramatic internal challenge to the regime).[91] It has also largely halted efforts to revitalize the Israeli-Syrian peace track as another way to distance Syria from Iran and align it with Western regional interests.

If domestic unrest continues, the current regime is likely to only increase its dependence on Iran as it finds itself more isolated regionally and internationally. Even if the Assad regime falls, a future Syrian regime will still share critical interests with Iran, such as opposition to Kurdish separatism. Depending on the nature of the future government, Arab neighbors and Turkey might quickly attempt to court Syria, but it is doubtful that the Syrians would give up all economic, political, and military ties to Iran, even under a different leadership. A new Syrian regime might question why it should have a less robust relationship with Iran than Iran has with its other neighbors. If the unrest in Syria deteriorates into civil war, various domestic groups might be more desperate for Iranian assistance. In short, any number of future scenarios for Syria suggest that a complete break with Iran might prove difficult.

Still, even the Assad regime, and certainly any successor leadership reflecting popular aspirations, could find reasons to reduce ties to the Islamic Republic. Syria is a Sunni-majority population with strong secular currents. Looking to the past, Iran has not always supported the Assad regime, remaining silent after the 2007 Israeli military strike on Syria's al-Kabir nuclear site. Syria also broke ranks with Iran in 1991 when it joined the U.S.-brokered Madrid peace talks. If Assad falls, opposition groups might not look favorably on Syria's relationship with Iran, given Iran's own record of brutal repression at home.

---

[91] For a discussion of the "peeling" logic of moving Syria away from Iran and back into the Arab fold, see Fandy, 2008.

But, as long as Assad stays in power, the days of Western inducements—World Trade Organization (WTO) membership, technical assistance, an association agreement with the EU, greater access to foreign markets, foreign assistance packages—are over.[92] For the time being, Iran remains Syria's primary ally. There are many reasons that Assad's Syria would not likely break ties with Iran even if it had other partners available. The Iranian-Syrian alliance has proved durable for more than three decades, and the political, strategic, economic, and cultural ties between the two nations suggest that the relationship extends far beyond a tactical "marriage of convenience."[93] Syria was the only Arab state to align with Iran during the Iran-Iraq war, and the two countries have found similar value in pursuing anti-U.S. stances and supporting nonstate actors, such as Hizballah and HAMAS. President Bashar al-Assad moved Syria toward even closer alignment in recent years, supporting some Iranian regional policies, as well as Iran's nuclear ambitions. Syria and Iran agreed to a defense pact in 2006 and an additional military cooperation agreement the following year, including provisions for intelligence cooperation, equipment, and training for Syrian forces.[94] Iranian economic stakes in Syria have also increased in recent years, with estimates of $1 billion to $3 billion in new investments.[95] Moreover, the regime might find value in joining Iran in its support to Hizballah because provoking Israel is a useful dis-

---

[92] For further discussion of such initiatives, see Kaplan, 2008.

[93] For an overview of the deep ties between Iran and Syria, see Yacoubian, 2007. Also see Lawson, 2007.

[94] Bilal Y. Saab argues, for example, that Arab and Israeli defense experts exaggerated the significance of the Iranian-Syrian defense pact, which, in his view, was

> mostly intended to send a political message to Washington that Tehran and Damascus are anything but isolated. . . ." As he notes, "Although Iran may supply Syria with low-level weaponry . . . it is unlikely to equip Syrian forces with advanced military hardware. . . . [T]he Islamic Republic knows that supplying Syria with strategic and ballistic missiles would be highly provocative to Israel, which is not in Iran's interest at this time. (Saab, 2006)

[95] See Yacoubian, 2007.

traction from troubles at home. As one analyst puts it, "There's nothing like a good war to stabilize an unstable regime."[96]

For the time being, U.S. leverage over Syria's Iran policies is limited. Even attempts to leverage areas of common interest, such as addressing the Iraqi refugee challenge (Syria hosts the largest Iraqi displaced population outside Iraq)[97] or reducing the flow of violent extremists across the Syrian border with Iraq, will be difficult if the Syrian repression continues. If a new regime emerges that is open to cooperation with the West, renewed efforts to build on these common interests, as well as the Syrian-Israeli peace process, could proceed.

Iraq

The fall of Saddam Hussein and the ensuing insurgency transformed Iraq from a regional power to a temporarily impotent object of competition among neighboring states. The 2010 formation of an Iraqi government with strong ties to Iran's theocracy increased fears of an ultimate Iranian "victory" in this contest among regional U.S. allies, such as Saudi Arabia and the smaller GCC states; the alignment of the Persian Gulf's two Shi'a-led states could potentially tip the Persian Gulf's geopolitical balance. However, a weak Iraq that acts as an Iranian "proxy" is hardly a foregone conclusion. Ethnicity, language, and even religious beliefs form natural barriers to greater Iranian influence in Iraq. The development of a potentially more democratic and less sectarian Iraqi state could eventually weaken Iran's position.

---

[96] Baer, 2008.

[97] Refugee numbers are unreliable and difficult to estimate for many reasons. For example, Iraqis who are illegally in neighboring countries fear discovery; not all estimates count Iraqis who left the country before 2003; some Iraqis travel to Jordan and Syria regularly for business and personal reasons, and it is difficult to disaggregate their numbers from those fleeing conflict; and most Iraqis who have fled do not wish to be referred to as "refugees." For estimates of the Iraqi refugee population, see United Nations High Commissioner for Refugees (UNHCR), 2007. A 2010 UNHCR survey found that most Iraqi refugees in Syria are reluctant to return home permanently (UNHCR, 2010).

The 2010 Iraqi government formation process demonstrated significant Iranian influence in Iraqi politics. Former prime minister Iyad Alawi's Al-Iraqiya coalition managed to win a plurality of seats, yet it was prevented from taking the first shot at forming a government. The next biggest winner, Prime Minister Nouri Al-Maliki's State of Law coalition, was initially unable to garner enough support to form a government. In particular, Moqtada al-Sadr, residing in the Iranian holy city of Qom at that time, objected to Maliki as prime minister. It appears that Iran's pressure on al-Sadr might have finally persuaded him to back Maliki as prime minister, facilitating the creation of a "unified" Shi'a-dominated government, a key Iranian objective.[98] The Sunnis, many of whom voted for Alawi, are viewed as Baathists by Iran, and Iraqi Sunni figures were given a nominal role in government. Jalaal Talabani, reelected president, also maintains close ties to Tehran. These developments fed Sunni Arab states' fears of a Shi'a "crescent" stretching from Iran through Iraq, Syria, and Lebanon.

The reality might be quite different, however. Iran's political influence is constrained by traditional Arab and Kurdish Iraqi suspicion of Persian Iran and by the historical enmity between the two nations, as demonstrated by the Iran-Iraq War. The Iraqi holy cities of Najaf and Karbala might also emerge in time to challenge Qom's influence as a religious center of the Shi'a world.[99] The Islamic Republic's system of *velayat-e faghih* (rule of the Supreme Jurisprudent) does not have many adherents across the border; Iran's theocracy is unlikely to serve as a model for the emerging Iraqi political system. The Iraqi government and Maliki in particular have hardly proven pliable partners for Iran. In June 2011, Maliki again cracked down on Iranian-backed militias affiliated with the remnants of Moqtada al-Sadr's Jaysh al-Mahdi.[100]

---

[98] "Moqtada al Sadr," 2010.

[99] Since 2003, much speculation has been made about the potential impact in Iran of reemerging Shi'a centers of theology in Karbala and Najaf. However, this influence has not materialized as expected, given Grand Ayatollah Sistani's eschewment of politics (and his network remains in Qom) and Iran's skill at managing and penetrating the Iraqi Shi'a clerical community. For further details regarding the Iranian-Iraqi relationship, see Wehrey, Thaler, et al., 2009; Slavin, 2008; and Khalaji, 2006.

[100]Schmidt, 2011.

It is even possible that Iraq can significantly threaten Iran's quest for regional power; Iraq might one day challenge Iran's role as a major OPEC oil producer, for example.[101] Iraq's potential rise and divergence from Iranian interests could, of course, precipitate more-active Iranian intervention in Iraqi affairs. Given its sectarian fissures and weak institutions, Iraq is unlikely to play a critical role as a U.S. ally in a regional approach to containing Iran. It will likely exist for some time as a contested arena where the United States and its Sunni Arab allies vie for influence with the Islamic Republic. The willingness of the Baghdad regime to support the United States is contingent on which faction is in power, its sympathies toward Iran, and its confidence about public support for pro-U.S. policies. Iraq would not support a U.S. or Israeli military action against Iran and would strongly object to the use of its airspace to conduct such an attack. Indeed, such an action could precipitate a significant Iraqi shift toward Tehran and away from Washington.

China

Given the importance of China's economic growth as the source of its domestic stability and emerging power, China has a strong interest in promoting regional stability in order to protect the flow of Chinese exports to the region, as well as the import of Middle East oil and gas to China. China's relations with Iran are shaped by this general interest.

From China's vantage point, Iran is an important energy source that is strategically located for the delivery of oil and gas to the Chinese market.[102] Moreover, because Iran is outside the U.S. orbit, China's interest in Iranian resources need not take a back seat to U.S. demand. From the Iranian perspective, China represents a growing market for

---

[101] Swartz and Faucon, 2010.

[102] China's interests transcend energy, however. China appears to view Iran as a secure source of energy in the event of a United States–China confrontation; Iran has also emerged as an important market for Chinese goods.

its oil and gas output and, given China's ambivalence to sanctioning Iran for its nuclear ambitions, a potential conduit for Iranian oil should the West move to freeze Iranian energy imports.

The economic ties between China and Iran are already considerable and likely to grow. Iran, along with Saudi Arabia and Angola, provide the largest share of Chinese oil imports.[103] China is also the second-largest importer of Iranian oil and, by extension, an important source of foreign currency for the regime in Tehran.[104] Economic cooperation has increased considerably in the aftermath of the Iraq war insofar as China has looked to Iran to pick up the slack in Iraqi production. In March 2004, China's state-owned oil trading company, Zhuhai Zhenrong Corporation, signed a 25-year deal to import 110 million tons of liquefied natural gas (LNG) from Iran.[105] In December 2007, China and Iran finalized a $2 billion deal awarding Sinopec the right to develop the Yadavaran field in Iran. In addition, China National Offshore Oil Corporation (CNOOC) signed a preliminary gas deal to develop Iran's North Pars Gas Field.[106] Chinese investment in Iran's energy sector is projected to exceed $100 billion over the next 25 years.[107] China also concluded a deal with Iran in 2009 to construct 20 nuclear power plants, even though the United States had asked China to halt trade in goods related to nuclear technology.[108]

China has shown some willingness to support Western efforts to sanction Iran for refusing to suspend uranium enrichment, as demonstrated by its support for UN Security Council resolution (UNSCR) 1929 (2010).[109] However, China has, in the past, blocked United States–led efforts to pursue additional UN sanctions against Iran and has consistently advocated a negotiated solution to the nuclear

---

[103] U.S. Energy Information Administration, 2010a.

[104] U.S. Energy Information Administration, 2010b.

[105] Gundzik, 2005.

[106] "CNOOC Confirms Preliminary Gas Deal with Iran," 2006.

[107] Leverett and Bader, 2005–2006, p. 191.

[108] Shenna, 2010, p. 355.

[109] UN Security Council, 2010.

issue. Not surprisingly, China favored the nuclear swap deal negotiated by Brazil and Turkey and expressed support for non-Western powers' involvement in negotiation efforts to resolve the nuclear dispute. As one Chinese arms-control official stated, "The recent tripartite agreement on nuclear material swapping among Iran, Turkey and Brazil shows that influential countries other than major Western powers have started helping resolve sensitive global issues. Such efforts should be applauded and encouraged. . . ."[110]

China has conditioned its support for sanctions against Iran on reassurances from other producers (e.g., Saudi Arabia, the UAE) that they would compensate for potential shortfalls caused by the disruption of Iranian supply. So, although China supports the U.S. position opposed to a nuclear-armed Iran (largely because of concerns about its effect on regional stability), it has consistently expressed reservations about U.S. tactics emphasizing isolation rather than engagement as the best means to resolve the nuclear dispute.

The main U.S. leverage with China regarding Iran derives from China's concern about continued unimpeded access to Middle Eastern oil. China can be induced to support measures that enhance stability in that region and will oppose those that risk any significant interruption in supply. Thus China would oppose an Israeli or U.S. military attack on Iran and would become a more difficult partner on sanctions and other measures to isolate Iran were such to occur.

Russia

Although Russia has significant energy and economic interests in the Middle East and Iran, its interests are distinct from those of other extraregional actors, such as China, in that it has adequate energy resources of its own and, in fact, profits from disruptions in supply elsewhere. Russia's energy holdings include the largest natural-gas reserves in the world, the second-largest coal reserves, and the eighth-largest oil

---

[110] Shenna, 2010.

reserves.[111] Russia's natural resource endowments give it a vested interest in keeping prices high and, thus, within limits, in a risk premium on the international price of oil.

Russia and Iran control more than 40 percent of the world's known gas reserves, and each country has a track record of using energy as a lever of foreign policy, albeit not with any great success. Russia has been a leader in bringing together the major gas producers under a single umbrella, the Gas Exporting Countries Forum (GECF), considered the initial step toward the establishment of a formal cartel. And, although the organization is still in its infancy, it has met with favorable reactions from representatives of Russia, Iran, Qatar, Algeria, Venezuela, and other important exporters. However, it is believed that the establishment of a functioning gas cartel is still ten to 15 years away, and there are important characteristics of gas production and export that would constrain the effectiveness of such a cartel.[112]

The relationship between Moscow and Tehran is characterized by a mix of cooperation that reflects the countries' shared interests and competition that grows out of each state's ambitions and perception of its weight in regional affairs.[113]

In terms of cooperation, Russia has done much to further Iran's nuclear program. This includes the supply of material, such as Russia's 2006 delivery of 82 tons of commercial-grade enriched uranium, as well as technical support, such as Russia's work on building the nuclear reactor at Bushehr. Russia is also one of the largest suppliers of heavy engineering products, high-tech goods, and military equipment to Iran, exporting $3.3 billion in goods in 2008 alone.[114] In addition to energy and economic interests, Russia shares with Iran an interest in limiting U.S. influence in Central Asia and the Caucasus and in stemming Sunni extremism in these areas.[115]

---

[111] U.S. Energy Information Administration, 2010c.

[112] Qadura, 2008.

[113] Shaffer, 2001; M. Katz, 2008.

[114] Shenna, 2010.

[115] Shenna, 2010.

In 2010, Russia demonstrated greater willingness to pressure Iran after the disclosure of the secret nuclear enrichment facility in Qom, supporting UNSCR 1929 (2010) and freezing its sale of the S-300 air defense system to Iran. Thus, although Russia (and China) have shown less resolve than their Western counterparts in confronting Tehran, Russia has voted numerous times in the Security Council for measures that called for a halt to Iranian enrichment and greater transparency from Tehran regarding its nuclear program.

Russia uses its relationship with Iran as a point of leverage in its dealings with the United States. By the same token, President Obama used his "reset" of relations with Russia to secure more Russian support for pressure on Iran in implicit exchange for moves by Washington to relax pressures for further North Atlantic Treaty Organization (NATO) expansion and alterations in U.S. plans for deployment of a Europe-wide anti–ballistic-missile field. Arguably, both those policy moves were desirable on their own merits, but they definitely helped move Russian policy on Iran as well.

As argued persuasively by Mark Katz, Russia's on-again, off-again support to Iran is consistent with a concerted effort by Moscow to cultivate Iranian dependence on Russia. In other words, Russia derives significant benefit by serving as a deterrent to any preemptive use of force against Iran and providing the regime access to material and technology. At the same time, Russia also secures advantages in its relationship with the United States by reason of its cooperation against Iran. By positioning itself as a pivotal actor capable of both enabling and halting Iran's nuclear program, Russia is maximizing its leverage vis-à-vis both Washington and Tehran.

However, Russia's capacity to play out this game depends, to some extent, on Iran's willingness to accept the role of a dependent state, given its often-assertive and independent regional policies.[116] Iran, for example, has refused to rely on Russia as its sole source of nuclear material and is instead pursuing enrichment activities of its own. In another act of defiance, Tehran has showed its independence from Russia in its

---

[116] Ghali, 2007.

positions on the demarcation of the Caspian Sea as it relates both to drilling and to the construction of Central Asian pipelines.[117]

Thus, in contrast to more-alarmist portrayals of Russian-Iranian alignment, the relationship is far more nuanced. Russia and Iran do have shared interests that drive limited cooperation in the spheres of energy and security. However, the two states also have competing visions of the balance of power in the Middle East and Central Asia. Iran has astutely used its relationship with Russia as added leverage in its dealings with the West, but it has bucked at accepting Russian dominance in regional affairs. Given Iran's self-assurance that it has become a serious regional power, tension in the Russian-Iranian relationship is likely to persist, serving as an important source of leverage for the United States in maintaining Russian pressure on Iran regarding its nuclear program.

Russia could prove less willing to support increased pressure on Iran if the United States and Israel were to strike Iran's nuclear facilities. Indeed, Russia is unnerved by unrest in Arab countries, such as Libya; the NATO-led military campaign in Libya contradicts Russia's traditional resistance to humanitarian interventions. Such developments have already led to more-cautious Russian positions on tougher measures against Iran.[118] In the event of a U.S. or Israeli military strike on Iranian nuclear facilities, Moscow would be unlikely to support new sanctions and less willing to adhere to those already in existence.

Europe

Europe's relations with Iran have been fraught with tension since the Islamic revolution of 1979. Iran's pursuit of a potential nuclear weapon capability is the most recent and greatest source of friction between the Islamic Republic and European powers, such as the United Kingdom, France, and Germany. However, Iran's strained diplomatic relations with Europe have been tempered by relatively close commercial rela-

---

[117] M. Katz, 2008, pp. 206, 209–210.

[118] See, for example, M. Katz, 2011.

tions, explaining, in part, the initial European hesitation to fully support U.S. policies toward Iran on the nuclear program.[119] The European approach toward Iran under the Khatami government was largely characterized by continued engagement without significant economic and political pressure. The EU maintained a relatively independent stance, serving as a mediator between the United States and Iran. However, the EU approach toward Iran since 2008 has been much more consistent with U.S. policy toward the Islamic Republic. The 2009 Iranian presidential election and the ensuing repression, in addition to Iran's nuclear policies, led to enhanced UN and European sanctions against Iran in 2010, which might have led the Iranian government to come back to the negotiation table in December of that year.

The Islamic Revolution severed Iran's historic relationship with not only the United States but the United Kingdom as well. Iran's revolutionaries viewed Europe with deep suspicion, especially given UK support for the shah. The regime's assassination of Iranian dissidents seeking refuge in Europe further strained relations. However, Iran's approach toward Europe began to change after Ayatollah Khomeini's death in 1989. Rafsanjani's attempts to lessen Iran's isolation and fashion a pragmatic policy toward Europe bore some fruit, though the Mikonos assassinations of Iranian dissidents led to a temporary deterioration in relations. European-Iranian ties began to blossom under President Khatami, whose political objectives and rhetoric appealed to European powers. Full relations between Iran and the United Kingdom were restored in 1999; Germany, France, and Italy also strengthened their respective diplomatic and economic ties with the Islamic Republic. Significant European investments in Iran's energy sector followed, along with Iranian access to much-needed European goods and technology. Iran's assassination of Europe-based opposition figures had effectively ceased by the 1990s.

The thawing of relations between Iran and the EU facilitated the latter's initial role as a relatively "independent" mediator on the nuclear program. The Europeans' interests in Iran were of a more commercial nature; unlike the United States, the EU was not a guarantor of regional

---

[119] Posch, 2010.

security and did not maintain a significant military presence in the Persian Gulf. The U.S. invasion of Iraq and subsequent U.S.-European tensions might have also limited European support for tougher U.S. policies against Iran. However, the Ahmadinejad government's more assertive stance on the nuclear program and the EU's inability to stop the nuclear program through engagement have resulted in a tougher European stand, culminating in support for UNSCR 1929 (2010) and much stronger supplementary European sanctions against Iran.

European-Iranian trade and overall relations have declined substantially since 2008. Europe's policy toward Iran is now mostly focused on the nuclear program, with the objective of preventing weaponization and containing Iran in case it develops a weapon capability.[120] Europe's support of U.S. policy on Iran, including harsher sanctions, has led to Iran's increased isolation and damage to its economy. However, the EU's policies on the nuclear program, especially support for sanctions, might have also hurt the EU's ability to wield influence in Iran on other issues of importance to Europe in the near and distant future. Europe's weakening ties with Iran allow emerging powers, such as China, to wield greater influence. A Europe hungry for energy and facing Chinese and Russian competition might not be willing to forgo economic cooperation with Iran indefinitely.

The UK and particularly France might support, or at least not condemn, a U.S. or Israeli strike on Iranian nuclear facilities. Germany would be more critical, and other European states would range along that spectrum. Further concerted European action against Iran would be much more difficult to secure in the aftermath of such an attack.

Conclusion

Regional states and global powers are united in opposing the Iranian nuclear program, but few with the concentration that marks U.S. policy. For most governments (i.e., those other than Israel) the nuclear program is one consideration among many regarding Iran. The Obama

---

[120]There is also a growing European focus on the regime's human rights abuses.

administration has, nevertheless, been quite successful in securing broad, although not universal, international support for sanctions on Iran, but this coalition remains fragile and probably cannot be led too much further absent some new Iranian provocation.

Iran's immediate neighbors are as antipathetic to U.S. aspirations for their political evolution as they are to Iranian goals. Most will resist the domestic reforms that offer the best antidote to Iranian influence, and they will offer little support for U.S. efforts to promote democratization in that country.

Regional governments are more worried about Iranian subversion than about Iranian invasion. The opportunities for such would increase in the wake of an unprovoked Israeli or U.S. attack on Iran. These governments are thus either opposed to or ambivalent about such a possibility, recognizing the sympathy for Iran that such a strike would engender among their own populations and the strain it would put on their relations with the United States.

One can only speculate, at this early stage, what the advent of more–popularly based governments throughout the Arab world might mean for U.S.-Iranian relations. The Iranian leadership professes to believe that the Arab Spring will ultimately redound to Iran's benefit. Other observers argue that the United States will gain and Iran lose influence as the result of democratization. Perhaps the most likely result of these ongoing events is a loss of influence for both Iran and the United States.

Iran has nothing to offer the democratizing regimes of the Arab world, either as a model or as a source of assistance. Tehran's main source of leverage in the Arab world has been its capacity to undermine the legitimacy of authoritarian regimes linked to Washington and, by association, to Israel. Popularly based Arab regimes will reduce those links and therefore be less vulnerable to that kind of subversion. They will be less dependent on the United States, less friendly to Israel, and, consequently, less vulnerable to Iranian propaganda. They might become less hostile to Tehran but also less concerned about its ability to appeal directly to their publics.

For the Gulf monarchies, on the other hand, the Arab Spring and its threat to their own stability will only increase their fear of the ideological challenge posed not just by Iran but also by democratizing Arab states and U.S. support for that process. These regimes will thus become more wary in their relations with both Tehran and Washington.

Syria might be an exception to this pattern of regional distancing both from Tehran and Washington. A more popularly based Syrian regime could loosen its ties to Tehran while strengthening relations with the United States.

CHAPTER FIVE

U.S. Instruments and Iranian Vulnerabilities

The United States possesses multiple means by which to influence Iran's internal and external behavior. They include diplomacy, sanctions, covert action, soft power, and military force. All of these have been employed in the past, not always to optimum effect. Iran is vulnerable to each to a varying degree.

Diplomacy

Intermittent and somewhat half-hearted engagement between Washington and Tehran has so far failed to resolve core differences between the two. There are several explanations. Some analysts argue that the United States and its allies have not been forthcoming enough in offering Iran a "grand bargain" that extends beyond the nuclear dispute by recognizing Iran's regional role and accepting its current form of government. In this view, the continued U.S. focus on sanctions and isolation has closed the door on viable engagement with Tehran. Others believe that the Iranians, particularly with the consolidation of principlist power, are simply not interested in a negotiated settlement on the nuclear file or any other issue of regional concern. Normalization of ties with the United States would threaten the ideological underpinnings of the regime and thus be ultimately rejected by the Supreme Leader.[1]

Regardless of the reasons for failure, diplomacy will remain an essential element in the U.S. toolkit. At a minimum, it is a necessary prelude to military action or expanded sanctions. Thus, although periods of high tension or intransigent Iranian behavior might, at times, suspend dialogue, the United States will be likely to continue some form of engagement effort.

A brief examination of previous diplomatic efforts toward Iran could shed light on future possibilities and continuing impediments to an engagement approach with Iran. Such efforts have fallen into three broad categories: indirect intermediaries, multilateral talks, and direct U.S.-Iranian engagement. Although distinct, the three approaches to engagement can complement one another and, in practice, have operated simultaneously. Of the three, the multilateral approach has proven the most active track, but its focus is largely limited to the nuclear file. Non-Western powers appear more interested in serving as intermediaries than they have in the past, suggesting that this type of engagement could become more common. Direct U.S.-Iranian dialogue has been relatively rare, and current political trends in both countries suggest that a dramatic breakthrough in U.S.-Iranian relations is unlikely in the short term. But, although direct dialogue might prove most difficult, it has the greatest potential to address the full range of U.S. interests vis-à-vis Iran and might be the only form of engagement that could lead to true rapprochement.

Third-Party Intermediaries

In the absence of official diplomatic ties with Iran, ruptured in 1980, third-party intermediaries have proved an important source for U.S.-Iranian communication and deal making. Although some such efforts have been successful in resolving disputes, starting with Algeria's mediation in 1980–1981 to end the hostage crisis, other experiences, notably

---

[1] For an extensive assessment of Iranian views and positions toward engagement with the United States, including differences among Iranian factions and leaders, see International Crisis Group, 2009.

the Iran-Contra affair, ended less favorably.[2] Another example of an indirect negotiation attempt occurred in 2003, when Iran transmitted a proposal to the United States through the Swiss that offered to open discussions on all outstanding issues, including the Arab-Israeli peace process.[3] Feeling emboldened by its early success in Afghanistan and Iraq (the chaos and violence that developed in the years thereafter had not yet unfolded), the United States ignored the offer. As former U.S. diplomat John Limbert argues, "By all accounts, that 2003 decision came from the illusory euphoria of easy military victory in Iraq and the view, popular with some in Washington at the time, that 'real men go to Tehran in tanks.'"[4]

The EU began a "comprehensive dialogue" with Iran in 2002 (addressing not only WMD but also human rights, terrorism, and the peace process) but, by 2003, reached a deadlock on these issues.[5] This led to the emergence of the "EU 3" (France, Germany, and Britain) and a focus exclusively on the nuclear issue, part of an effort to support U.S. pressure on Iran to reverse its enrichment activities. Although the initiative was a significant achievement for European unity efforts, it did little to resolve the nuclear dispute and satisfy U.S. concerns. The United States joined these talks late in the George W. Bush administration, as did Russia and China, but to no great effect.

A more recent trend in diplomacy with Iran has begun to involve non-Western powers interested in serving as intermediaries between the West and Iran to resolve the nuclear dispute. Turkey and Brazil attempted to renegotiate an arrangement initially offered the United States, among others, that Iran had at first favored but quickly backed out of. This deal would have transferred Iranian low-enriched uranium out of the country in return for fuel rods for Iran's medical reactor. But the United States and other Western powers rejected Turkey and Bra-

---

[2]   See Limbert, 2008, p. 7. In this case, the United States secretly relied on Iranian intermediaries with questionable authority to represent Iranian authorities in the attempt to trade U.S. weapons for the release of U.S. hostages held in Lebanon.

[3]   See Leverett, 2006. Also see Kessler, 2006.

[4]   Limbert, 2008, p. 2.

[5]   See Dalton, 2009.

zil's mediation efforts, arguing that the terms had become too favorable to Iran by the time the renewed arrangement had been negotiated.[6]

This episode led to increased tension between the United States, Turkey, and Brazil and a U.S. preference to continue pressing nuclear negotiations through broader multilateral forums, most significantly the UN P5+1 process. Nonetheless, because non-Western powers increasingly view themselves as pivotal regional and international players, it would not be surprising if such actors continue to find ways to insert themselves as intermediaries in the future, particularly if the P5+1 channel remains at an impasse.

Multilateral Diplomacy

The U.S. involvement in multilateral talks with Iran on the nuclear file began in July 2008 with the P5+1 talks in Geneva and again in October 2009. The talks focused on incentives (e.g., new aircraft, access to the United States on other issues of concern) that could convince Iran to suspend its uranium-enrichment efforts, complementing the pressure applied against Iran through sanctions. Given widespread support within Iran for the right to enrich uranium, Iran rejected such incentives, leading some analysts to argue that suspension was an unrealistic goal and the West should instead pursue intrusive transparency measures and inspections by the IAEA to ensure that the enriched uranium was not diverted to military use.[7]

More-recent P5+1 negotiations with Iran have focused on fuel swaps and inspections, but the goal of zero enrichment remains, resulting in the standoff with Iran. The discovery of a second, hitherto undeclared Iranian enrichment plant near Qom in the fall of 2009 and the failure of multilateral negotiations to date led to the ratcheting up of sanctions, culminating in UNSCR 1929 in June 2010. These UN sanctions were followed by additional sanctions imposed unilaterally by the EU, Canada, Australia, South Korea, and Japan. Another round of talks took place in late 2010, again in Geneva. The parties continued talks in January 2011 in Istanbul, where the focus was on the nuclear-

---

[6]   Borger, 2011.

[7]   See, for example, Takeyh, 2008.

enrichment swap deal that was eventually rejected by the Iranians, only to be later revivified by Brazil and Turkey and then rejected by the United States.

Direct U.S.-Iranian Dialogue

The history of attempts at direct dialogue between the United States and Iran represents a series of missed opportunities. Whenever one side seemed ready to talk seriously, the other was not. Both sides face significant domestic political constraints to engagement with the other and, in Iran's case, ideological impediments as well. The legacy of mistrust and conflict between the two countries for the past 30 years will be difficult to reverse because animosities and grievances run deep. Moreover, U.S. regional allies—the Arab states and Israel—are wary of U.S.-Iranian rapprochement, fearing that normalization will undermine their own relationships with Washington and signal acceptance of Iran as a dominant regional power at their expense.

Still, given the stakes and a range of shared interests, and the limitations of other types of engagement efforts, successive U.S. administrations have attempted direct dialogue with Iran despite the absence of official relations. As previously mentioned, some of these efforts were secret (e.g., the Iran-Contra scandal of the 1980s). But other efforts were more public, with the Clinton administration attempting to capitalize on the election of the reformist Iranian president Mohammad Khatami in 1997 by increasing visible, albeit minor, confidence-building measures.[8] Following the September 11th attacks, U.S. diplomats directly engaged with Iranian officials in the context of the UN-sponsored Bonn conference to stabilize Afghanistan and form a new government, but Washington subsequently ignored Iranian interest in continuing and expanding that cooperation.[9]

In the second George W. Bush administration, U.S. Iran policy shifted and contact was again attempted in response to a deteriorating security situation and the release of a prominent bipartisan report, by

---

[8]   For a detailed account of such measures, see International Crisis Group, 2009.

[9]   See Dobbins, 2008.

the Iraq Study Group, which called for engagement with Iran.[10] In May and July 2007, the U.S. ambassador to Iraq, Ryan Crocker, engaged in direct, official talks with his Iranian counterpart in Baghdad, focused on stabilizing Iraq. Although the limited talks were quite confrontational and did not produce any obvious results, they demonstrated a clear shift in tactics by the Bush administration; talk of military action against Iran diminished. Subsequently, Iranian-inspired attacks on U.S. forces in Iraq decreased. Unofficial, track two dialogues on the nuclear issue also continued during this period, including a series of meetings between former Defense Secretary William Perry and other high-level U.S. nuclear-nonproliferation and Iran experts with Iranian officials in European cities.[11]

The election of President Obama, who, during his campaign, advocated greater dialogue with adversaries, only raised greater expectations about the prospects for substantive and sustained U.S.-Iranian engagement. An important speech by Iran's Supreme Leader in 2008 also indicated that engagement with the United States was acceptable if it served Iranian interests, and a letter by Iranian president Ahmadinejad congratulating President Obama after the election seemed to reinforce such views.[12]

President Obama signaled early in his administration that he was prepared to talk with the Iranians without preconditions, departing from the previous administration's policy of making uranium-enrichment suspension a precondition for general talks. In the early months of the Obama administration, the United States invited Iran to a March 2009 multilateral meeting on Afghanistan. President Obama's rhetoric of an "unclenched fist" and his Norouz message to the Iranian people and government suggested that the United States was not interested in regime change but in different Iranian behavior and a new type of U.S.-Iranian relationship. The Obama administration's efforts to reach out to Tehran proved tactically clumsy. Instead of responding to President Ahmadinejad's letter of congratulations on his election, Obama

---

[10]   For a brief overview of engagement efforts in the Bush administration, see Singh, 2009.

[11]   See Rozen, 2009. Also see Kralev and Slavin, 2009.

[12]   International Crisis Group, 2009, p. 5.

chose to address himself to the Supreme Leader, who proved less interested in initiating such a dialogue. Instead of authorizing U.S. diplomats to quietly engage their Iranian colleagues in such places as Kabul, Baghdad, and New York, the administration announced its intention to invite Iranian ambassadors to U.S. embassy July 4 parties around the world, only to reverse itself and withdraw the invitations a few days later, in reaction to the controversy over the just-concluded Iranian presidential elections.[13]

President Obama's efforts to reach out to the Iranians failed to receive a positive response.[14] Some analysts argue that the Obama administration's engagement efforts have lacked sincerity and have been overshadowed by continued policies focused on pressure and isolation.[15] Whether the Obama initiatives were insufficiently sincere or just tactically inept, the result was that, like previous attempts, they have so far failed to produce any sustained or significant process. The tumultuous Iranian elections of June 2009 further complicated prospects for productive direct U.S.-Iranian diplomacy, increasing the domestic political costs, on both sides, of any effort at rapprochement.[16]

Some continue to argue that the only way to undercut the consolidation of hard-liners in Tehran and "promote political decompression in Iran" is to continue to pursue direct engagement and, ultimately, détente with the Islamic Republic.[17] The political trends in both the United States and Iran do not appear promising for such engagement, even on limited issues of common concern, such as Iraq, Afghanistan, or Sunni extremists. And the regional and practical impediments of how to engage Iran remain (e.g., *whom* should the United States

---

[13] Kessler, 2009.

[14] Solomon, 2009.

[15] Leverett and Leverett, 2010.

[16] The June elections also led to an internal debate within the administration about its Iran policy. See Cohen, 2009. On the implications that the Iranian elections could have for U.S. policy, see Sadjadpour, 2009.

[17] Brumberg and Blechman, 2010.

engage?).[18] The Iranian regime's conception of its interests and the marginalization of more-pragmatic factions will limit prospects for bilateral diplomacy for some time to come.

Iran's Political System and U.S. Diplomacy

The 2009 Iranian presidential election only reinforced the regime's suspicions of the United States and might have closed the window on any early opportunities for meaningful negotiations between the two nations, weakening the U.S. ability to engage the Islamic Republic.

The 2009 election laid bare elite and popular divisions within Iran. Broadly speaking, the political system has been split into two opposing camps, the conservatives/principlists and the reformists/pragmatic conservatives. Conservatives and principlists such as Khamenei, Ahmadinejad, and the top echelon of the Revolutionary Guards, viewed the election as an opportunity to fundamentally refashion the Islamic Republic and its revolutionary ideals. Hence, they portrayed the Green Movement as a U.S.-sponsored fifth column. Linking the Green Movement with the United States might have enhanced Khamenei's standing among his base of conservative supporters and helped justify the subsequent crackdown on the opposition. However, Khamenei and his inner circle appear to genuinely believe in the threat of a velvet revolution that would destroy the Islamic Republic. In their view, the United States, having failed to defeat Iran and dominate the Middle East militarily, seeks to overthrow the Islamic Republic through cultural and "psychological" warfare.

The reformists and the Green Movement, on the other hand, believe that Iran's myriad social, political, and economic ills are a grave danger to the Islamic Republic, making reforms essential for the regime's long-term survival. The Green Movement is not, by nature, pro–United States. However, its political and economic interests might, to some extent, coincide with U.S. interests regarding Iran and

---

[18] One dilemma the United States faces is that President Ahmadinejad appears more enthusiastic about engagement than the Supreme Leader does but the Supreme Leader has the ultimate authority. On this question, see Khalaji, 2008, and Sadjadpour, 2008b.

the wider Middle East, thus enhancing U.S. leverage over an important sector of Iranian society.

The reformist/pragmatic conservative goal of creating a more open society and political system requires for success Iran's integration into the global economy. In the past, this view has led to Iranian foreign policies that were more amenable to Western and U.S. interests. In addition, the Green Movement and the pragmatic conservatives believe that the Ahmadinejad government's nuclear policy has damaged Iran's overall national security interests. Though such figures as Rafsanjani have historically supported the nuclear program, they might ultimately come to view Iran's current and future pursuit of a weapon capability as a great liability, particularly given the intense international pressure placed on the Islamic Republic. Responding to stronger sanctions against Iran, Rafsanjani has warned the regime not to treat sanctions as a "joke."[19] A potential compromise on the nuclear program, and better relations with the United States, might be viewed by the Green Movement and the pragmatic conservatives as safeguarding their vision for a viable Islamic Republic.

Some have argued that the United States should directly (if perhaps covertly) aid the Green Movement, or at least provide more-explicit rhetorical support. The Green Movement appears to be a semiunderground sociopolitical movement rather than an organized opposition political party. It does not seem to need or want external financial or logistical aid.[20] Moreover, U.S. moral support for the Green Movement could actually reinforce the regime's portrayal of the movement as a fifth column supported by an "imperial" power.

Sanctions

Iran has faced U.S. sanctions for the past three decades. In 1979, the United States froze billions of dollars of Iranian assets in response to

---

[19] Fassihi, 2010.

[20] Technological assistance allowing Iranians greater access to the external world could be important and does not have to come from the United States alone.

the seizure of the U.S. embassy and the holding of 52 Americans as Iranian hostages. In addition, the United States introduced sanctions that constrained U.S. commercial and business ties with the Islamic Republic. These sanctions did not completely prohibit trade; significant U.S.-Iranian bilateral commerce continued until the Clinton administration, when Iran's support for terrorism and its pursuit of nuclear capability resulted in stronger U.S. sanctions, including ILSA,[21] which penalized domestic and foreign companies investing more than $20 million in Iran's energy sector. The United States was concerned about antagonizing European and Asian allies that maintained significant trade and investment ties with the Islamic Republic, and ILSA's extra-territorial provisions were seldom enforced by the U.S. government. However, the revelation of Iran's nuclear facilities at Natanz and Arak in 2002 changed the heretofore largely unilateral nature of the sanction regime against Iran. Since that time, the Islamic Republic has come under growing international diplomatic and economic pressure to clarify the nature of its nuclear program.

The United States initially faced considerable resistance in fashioning a comprehensive and truly global sanction regime against the Islamic Republic. The 2003 U.S. decision to invade Iraq despite the opposition of nearly all regional states and many allies, and the subsequent failure to find any WMD, initially limited enthusiasm for sanctions against Iran's alleged nuclear weapon program. Hence, the initial three rounds of UN sanctions against Iran were relatively mild and had a limited effect on Iran's economy and nuclear decisionmaking. UN Security Council resolutions 1737, 1747, and 1803, respectively, called on member states to block Iran's import and export of "sensitive nuclear material and equipment" and to freeze the financial assets of those involved in Iran's nuclear activities; banned all of Iran's arms exports and arms exports to Iran; froze the assets and restricted the travel of people it deemed involved in the nuclear program; and *encouraged* scrutiny of the dealings of Iranian banks.[22] However, the resolu-

---

[21] Upon passage of the Iran Freedom Support Act (Pub. L. 109-293) in 2006, ILSA was renamed the Iran Sanctions Act because it no longer applied to Libya.

[22] UN Security Council, 2006a, 2007b, 2008b.

tions' specific targeting of Iran's nuclear program did little to effect its economy as a whole.

The United States sought to apply greater unilateral economic pressure against Iran despite the lack of comprehensive international sanctions. This included the strengthening of the Iran Sanctions Act in 2006 and the U.S. Treasury Department's designation of Iranian government entities, companies, and individuals involved with the nuclear and missile programs.[23] In addition, the United States barred Iranian banks and financial institutions from directly accessing the U.S. financial system through "U-turn" transactions.[24]

Iran's continued pursuit of a potential nuclear weapon capability has led to wider international pressure against the Islamic Republic since 2009. UN Security Council resolution 1929, supported by all permanent members of the Security Council, including China, significantly tightened sanctions, hindering Iran's use of the international financial system. UNSCR 1929 was specifically designed to enable follow-up measures by individual countries; subsequent sanctions against Iran by the United States, the EU, Australia, Japan, South Korea, and other states might have had a much greater impact on the Iranian economy than all UN resolutions combined. The U.S. Comprehensive Iran Sanctions, Accountability, and Divestment Act (CISADA) of 2010 authorizes the U.S. president to penalize foreign companies that seek to aid Iran's fuel-refinement capability or provide it with refined-fuel products. The act also authorizes sanctions against companies that invest in Iran's energy sector.[25] Given the change in allied opinion, the United States faces somewhat less resistance to the application of these extraterritorial measures, thus considerably enhancing their effect.

---

[23] Levitt, 2010.

[24] According to Levitt, 2010, "Iranian banks are prohibited from engaging in financial transactions with American banks under sanctions passed after the 1979 seizure of the U.S. embassy in Tehran. But U.S. banks had been allowed to process certain dollar transactions for Iranian entities simply for the purpose of clearing those transactions. This authorization was referred to as a U-turn exception."

[25] Pub. L. 111-195, 2010.

Banking restrictions have had a particularly negative effect on the Iranian economy. U.S. and international financial sanctions have made it difficult for Iranian companies to obtain letters of credit, raising the cost of business. The devaluation of Iran's currency in October 2010 might have been caused by the enforcement of harsher banking sanctions. In addition, the 2010 sanctions have resulted in the denial of coverage for the Islamic Republic of Iran Shipping Lines by international insurers. As a result, several Iranian ship owners have defaulted on their loans, and their ships have been impounded in international ports.[26] More broadly, many European and Asian countries have withdrawn from or reduced investments in Iran's vital energy sector. Key European energy firms, such as France's Total and Germany's Linde Group, have cut off ties completely. Japan also ended its involvement in the giant Azadegan oil field in October 2010.[27]

The 2010 sanctions have also affected Iran's trade relations with traditionally friendly partners, such as India. In December 2009, India's central bank decided that the Asian Clearing Union, based in Tehran, could no longer be used by Indian companies to pay for Iranian oil, disrupting important trade relations between the two countries.[28] The dispute with India could be particularly disturbing for Iran's leadership because the two nations have enjoyed close relations as members of the Non-Aligned Movement; Iran has also emphasized its relations with Eastern nations, such as India, as a means to bypass "Western" sanctions.

Iran's economy is arguably the regime's greatest source of weakness. Despite possessing some of the world's largest natural-gas and oil reserves, the country remains mired in inflation and unemployment. The anemic state of the economy in the past three decades has been one of the primary sources of public dissatisfaction with the regime. Future economic decline could lead to greater agitation among Iran's youth-

---

[26] "Iran Says Singapore Frees 3 Impounded Iranian Ships," 2011.

[27] Inajima, 2010.

[28] India has vacillated on enforcing this restriction, and some reports suggest that the Indian government has facilitated work-arounds to ease continuing trade. See Sharma, 2011.

ful, well-educated, yet endemically unemployed and underemployed population.

Iran's economic problems and loss of government revenue appear to have been key factors in driving the overhaul of the Islamic Republic's enormous subsidy system. Prior to reforms in 2010, the Iranian government spent up to $100 billion, or 25 percent of its gross domestic product (GDP), on subsidies for fuel, water, and food.[29] The subsidy system was created after the start of the Iran-Iraq War in order to mollify the beleaguered and restless masses. Subsidies have also been a key component of the regime's goal of correcting social and economic inequality. Nevertheless, the Iranian government has been well aware of the costs associated with subsidies; both Rafsanjani and Khatami sought to reform the system but were thwarted by factional opposition and domestic unrest.

Ahmadinejad, facing a declining economy and international sanctions, has taken the unprecedented step of reforming the subsidy system. The Iranian government aims to replace subsidies with cash handouts to the "neediest" Iranians; the cash payments, however, are temporary and meant to cushion the lower classes, presumably the regime's base of support, from the initial shock of the subsidy overhaul. In this respect, at least, sanctions have forced very positive, if highly unpopular, reform. As of 2011, the subsidy cuts have led to much higher fuel prices and strikes by Iranian truck drivers. A complete overhaul of the system could lead to massive unrest and violence against the regime in the next few years, weakening the support of Iran's lower religious classes.[30]

Sanctions might have affected Iranian decisionmaking by widening the cleavages within the political system. The Ahmadinejad government's failure to prevent stronger sanctions against Iran was strongly criticized by key political opponents within the conservative/principlist camp, including prominent figures, such as Rafsanjani. Iran's isolation and declining economy have been exploited by Ahmadinejad's principlist opponents, including parliamentary speaker Ali Larijani and chief

---

[29] Wright, 2010.

[30] Though there has been relatively little public backlash to date.

of the judiciary Ayatollah Sadeq Larijani. The two Larijani brothers, closely tied to Khamenei and Iran's powerful security establishment, are potential "successors" to the Ahmadinejad presidency. As Iran's lead nuclear negotiator, Ali Larijani pursued a more flexible nuclear policy that included consistent and, at times, fruitful engagement with the EU and the IAEA. He has consistently criticized Ahmadinejad's style of governance, as has Sadeq Larijani. A future Iranian government dominated by the two brothers might pursue somewhat different foreign and nuclear policies.

Furthermore, the regime's vulnerabilities might lead it to recalibrate its overall national security policies. Iran's declining economy, divided political system, and internal unrest might have prompted the regime to reengage the P5+1 in discussions held in Geneva in 2010 and Istanbul in 2011. However, Iran's willingness to engage the international community could be a sign of momentary weakness rather than a real desire to compromise due to domestic and international pressures and could signal a resolve to buy time while developing nuclear capabilities. The regime appears increasingly to perceive nuclear capability as a panacea for all internal and external problems, including internal unrest and the threat of U.S. regime change. Short- and medium-term economic and diplomatic costs would be well worth the future gains from nuclear weapon capability.

Covert Action

The United States has a history of covert action in Iran, including the 1953 coup against Mossadegh. The Islamic Republic has accused the United States of supporting various opposition and insurgent groups.[31] These include the Iraq-based Mujahedin-e Khalq Organization (MKO), the Green Movement, the Baluch terrorist group Jundullah, and the Kurdish group Free Life Party of Kurdistan (Partiya Jiyana Azad a Kurdistanê, or PJAK). The MKO, though on the U.S. list of terrorist groups, nevertheless enjoyed U.S. protection in post-Saddam

---

[31] Nader and Laha, 2011.

Iraq. Despite the Iranian regime's claims, there is little public evidence to suggest that the United States is supporting the Green Movement or various insurgent groups. Nevertheless, the option of supporting these groups does exist and has some attraction, given Iran's intransigence on the nuclear program, and some justification, given Iran's support of Iraqi and Afghan insurgents fighting U.S. forces.

The Iranian regime fears ethnic separatism. Though a Persian and Shi'a majority nation, Iran is nevertheless inhabited by Sunni ethnic groups, such as the Kurds and the Baluch. The Kurds make up as much as 10 percent of Iran's population and are concentrated in western and northwestern Iran. They have been marginalized and discriminated against since the shah's time, though they are probably better off than their brethren in Turkey and Syria. The Baluch are the most discriminated against of all Iranian ethnic groups. They inhabit Iran's southeastern province of Sistan va Baluchistan, which borders Afghanistan and Pakistan. The Ahmadinejad government has been particularly repressive of the Sunni Baluch, preventing them from practicing their religion freely.[32]

Kurdish and Baluch insurgents have waged a bloody campaign against the Iranian government; Jundullah, a Baluch movement, has assassinated several senior Revolutionary Guards officers. Potential U.S. financial and military support for Baluch and Kurdish insurgents could create greater instability for the regime and distract it from other pressing issues, such as dealing with the Green Movement (mostly based in Persian-majority urban areas) and improving Iran's economy.

However, U.S. support for Iranian insurgents could motivate the regime to increase material support to Iraqi and Afghan insurgents fighting U.S. and coalition forces. This already seems to be happening in Iraq, but Iran has, thus far, provided limited support to the Taliban, though the regime might decide to step up its training, funding, and arming of the Taliban in retaliation for U.S. covert actions.

U.S. support for Iranian insurgents could also hinder its overall objectives of influencing the Iranian regime and the wider population. Iranians, especially the Persian majority, are deeply suspicious

---

[32] Nader and Laha, 2011.

and resentful of Western intervention in Iran's affairs. Western association with ethnic minorities is often interpreted as an effort to break up the Iranian nation, as was the case with the British in the nineteenth century.

U.S. covert support for the MKO and the Green Movement will produce similar reactions among the Iranian population, assuming that it becomes known, as most U.S. covert actions seem to become. The MKO, still regarded by the United States (as well as Iran) as a terrorist organization, is widely disliked in Iran because of the support it received from and provided to Saddam Hussein during the Iran-Iraq War. U.S. support for the Green Movement will also result in it losing credibility, especially because the regime portrays it as a fifth column beholden to U.S. and Israeli interests. Even Iranians who oppose the regime might resent any sort of material U.S. support for Iranian opposition groups.

Covert action, whether by the United States or Israel, might be successful in slowing down the Iranian nuclear program but is unlikely to stop it. The Stuxnet virus appears to have inflicted significant damage on Iran's main facility at Natanz. The assassination of Iranian nuclear scientists, attributed by some to Israel, might encourage defections and damage morale among the Iranian scientific community. Nevertheless, Stuxnet and the assassinations might have had limited effect in slowing down Iran's program; they could also provoke retaliatory attacks and, if attributed to the United States, could undermine international support for overt pressures on Iran.[33] Such covert action might also have the unintended consequence of fortifying the regime's resolve in continuing the nuclear program.

Soft Power

Joseph Nye defines *soft power* as what a country can obtain "through attraction rather than coercion or payments. . . . [S]oft power arises from

---

[33] Warrick, 2011.

the attractiveness of a country's culture, political ideals, and policies."[34] Iranians tend to express admiration for the people of the United States. Moreover, Iranians respect U.S. technological, scientific, and even military achievements. The United States is the world's greatest power, a position that Iran once occupied, and, as John Limbert observes, Iranians "respect power." But Iranians across the political and ideological spectrum have mixed feelings toward the United States; positive attitudes regarding the American people and their achievements could be offset by hostile attitudes toward U.S. actions, for example. RAND's survey of Iranian public opinion has shown that most Iranians appear to have low opinions of the U.S. "government" and its policies toward Iran.[35]

The United States certainly appeals to segments of the Iranian population, and perhaps even individual members of the political elite, many of whom were educated in the United States before the revolution. U.S. popular culture also resonates among Iran's youthful population. Democracy and human rights, increasingly global rather than distinctly American values, also have strong appeal, as evidenced indeed by the democratic aspects of Iran's oddly hybrid constitution. It is these aspects that the Green Movement seeks to give greater prominence while maintaining loyalty to the theocratic content of the constitution as well.

U.S. soft power toward Iran can be exercised in several ways. The United States can serve as a role model to Iran and its population, potentially demonstrating how its democratic and relatively open society has led to economic, scientific, and technological advances.

The United States can also take a more direct and active approach to exercising its soft power. For example, Iran's information environment and media are closely controlled by the official Islamic Republic of Iran Broadcasting. This allows the Iranian government to shape public perceptions on myriad topics, including the United States. U.S. broadcasts to Iran can play an important role in reshaping Iranian attitudes and strengthening U.S. soft power. There is evidence to show

---

[34] Nye, 2004.

[35] Elson and Nader, 2011.

that Voice of America, in addition to other television and radio broad-casts, is popular in Iran and has played an important role in forming public perceptions since the 2009 Iranian presidential election.[36] Fur-thermore, social media, such as blogs, Facebook, and Twitter, played an important role in mobilizing the masses after the 2009 election and have remained the Green Movement's primary source of expression. The Iranian government has responded to this by extending its control of the Internet and using social media for its own political purposes. U.S. policies designed to loosen the regime's tight grip on the Internet and social media can not only empower the Iranian opposition but also improve perceptions of the United States.

Increased interaction between Americans and Iranians can also enhance U.S. soft power. The United States and Iran do not maintain any official diplomatic relations, making it difficult for U.S. diplomats to interact with their counterparts. Direct contacts between U.S. and Iranian diplomats can enhance U.S. public diplomacy efforts toward Iran, in addition to providing a window to the United States for Irani-ans with little access to external sources of information. Cultural, sci-entific, and sports exchanges between the two countries can also serve a similar purpose.

The United States possesses significant cultural and social influ-ence among the Iranian population. Some of this soft power is coun-tered by hostile attitudes toward the United States. In addition, the United States could face difficulties in defining the level of its soft power in Iran or in crafting very specific policies employing soft power. Regardless, the limitations of U.S. hard power (military and economic) and limited diplomatic leverage call for greater attention to the uses of U.S. soft power regarding Iran.

U.S. soft power is more likely to resonate among segments of the Iranian population than within the regime. Western cultural and political norms have permeated Iranian society in the past two centu-ries. The concepts of nationalism, democracy, and individual rights, for example, were powerful forces in shaping the 1905 constitutional

---

[36] Bahrampour, 2010.

revolution and Prime Minister Mossadegh's efforts to nationalize Iranian oil in the 1950s.

The Islamic Republic, though a theocracy, has not been immune to Western influences. The bifurcation of the regime into appointed and elected institutions reflects adherence to a republican system of government, however imperfect. Iranian elections have played an important role in shaping politics and policy, though Iranians' political role has been much more circumscribed than that of their Western counterparts. The Islamic Republic has become even less democratic since Ahmadinejad's election in 2005 and his reelection in 2009. Nevertheless, the regime's inability to completely crush the Green Movement demonstrates the resonance of democratic norms within Iranian society. Even more-junior elements of the religious establishment, one of the regime's main pillars of support, have shown a proclivity for the Green Movement, which combines Islamist governance with democratic principles.

However, the regime's top echelon is more susceptible to pressure through sanctions than through either direct diplomacy or cultural or social influences. The Green Movement's interests are more in line with U.S. interests. But the Green Movement does not have formal power, and its objective of reforming the existing political system—which could take years, if not decades, to achieve—might not satisfy U.S. interests in the near future. Hence, U.S. soft power is likely to be more effective with Iran's people than with its rulers.

The Military Option

Although the typical scenario for U.S. military action against Iran envisages conventional air strikes against Iran's nuclear facilities, other options exist along the continuum of military operations, including show-of-force operations in the Persian Gulf, cyberwarfare, and a broad-based air campaign against political and military targets. The utility of these options needs to be examined through the lens of U.S. main objectives: halting Iran's nuclear weapon program, moderating Iran's external behavior, and reforming its internal political system.

Halting Iran's Nuclear Program

The consensus among U.S. officials seems to be that a U.S. airstrike would delay but not completely destroy Iran's nuclear program, given the dispersed and protected nature of key facilities and the incomplete intelligence picture regarding the full extent of Iran's nuclear infrastructure.[37] Additionally, the regime might conclude that a limited airstrike against its nuclear enterprise is, in fact, a full-fledged attempt at regime change because the nuclear program is overseen by the Revolutionary Guards, which also serves as the regime's Praetorian Guard. This assumption could trigger a chain of escalatory responses that is beyond what U.S. planners might anticipate, including closure of the Strait of Hormuz, asymmetric attacks on U.S. and allied facilities in the Gulf and worldwide, and ballistic-missile salvos on civilian and military targets in the Gulf. Cyberattacks on Iranian nuclear facilities might do less damage but also might occasion a less violent reaction.

A key consideration for both options is that, although they might affect the *physical* aspects of Iran's nuclear program, it is unclear whether they will significantly alter the regime's *political* will and calculus about the necessity of the program. Indeed, such actions might, in fact, fortify the regime's resolve to redouble its efforts, both as a deterrent and for domestic political reasons, in order to close ranks among competing factions and to rally the populace.

Moderating Iranian External Behavior

Much of Iran's regional influence is exerted at the ideological, political, and soft-power levels. Military power is only one tool, and often not the most important, in containing this influence. However, there are military steps that will be important in bolstering local resistance to such Iranian efforts. These include strengthening the defenses of U.S. allies in the Gulf to provide reassurance and deterrence (focusing on air and coastal defense, counterair, and early warning) and assistance to friendly security forces in conflict zones where Iran's Qods force has supported nonstate actors. Such assistance would focus on the PA, the Iraqi security forces (ISF), and the Lebanese Armed Forces (LAF). In

---

[37] Carden, 2010; Stewart, 2010b.

addition to military aid, U.S. strategic communication can help shape local perceptions of Iranian influence by highlighting Iranian misdeeds and the malign effects of its lethal support to armed groups.[38]

Influencing Iran's Internal Evolution

A conventional military strike against the Islamic Republic would be unlikely to move that country's internal political dynamics in ways that are favorable to U.S. interests. Iran's embattled hard-liners have long attempted to bolster sagging support for the regime by cultivating a sense of siege among the public. A U.S. attack would likely enable them to further consolidate their control and close ranks with competing factions while undercutting more-pragmatic and more-conciliatory voices. In addition, the Iranian populace itself might evince greater support for the regime in a show of nationalism.[39] However, when employed over the long term as part of a broad-based diplomatic strategy of containment, military power might be able to produce fissures and debates among the elite about the opportunity costs of its isolation, possibly empowering more-pragmatic actors.

Conclusion

The United States will be able to exert only a modest level of influence on Iran in the short and medium terms. U.S. diplomatic leverage is constrained by the bitter history of U.S.-Iranian relations and the domestic legitimacy the regime derives from defying the United States. The 2009 Iranian presidential election and the resulting divisions within the political system and Iranian society at large have made the Islamic Republic even less susceptible to direct U.S. diplomatic influ-

---

[38] The clearest example of this occurred in mid- and late 2008 in Iraq, when U.S. military forces publicized Iran's military support to the so-called Special Groups and other Shi'a militias. This helped build popular Iraqi support for the Maliki government's campaign against these groups.

[39] Stewart, 2010b.

ence while also making it more vulnerable to U.S. economic leverage and soft power. The regime's conservative and principlist decisionmakers, ascendant in the postelection period, are unlikely to be swayed by U.S. efforts at engagement. However, the United States will continue to exercise considerable and perhaps increasing economic leverage over Iran in the next few years. U.S. and international sanctions against Iran, particularly CISADA and UNSCR 1929, have significantly undermined Iran's economy and might have widened divisions within the regime. At a minimum, economic and political sanctions very substantially limit Iran's ability to project power and influence, which is one prime objective of U.S. policy. Setbacks in the nuclear program itself, including the Stuxnet attack on Natanz and the assassination of Iranian nuclear scientists, might have slowed the nuclear program and possibly helped bring Iran to the negotiation table in 2010–2011. However, such covert actions, assuming that that is what these represent, and whoever may be responsible, probably strengthen Iran's resolve to continue the nuclear program.

The Iranian populace is more susceptible to U.S. influences on cultural and social matters than it is on political and national security issues. Iran's ideologically motivated drive to become economically, technologically, and militarily self-sufficient hinders U.S. economic and diplomatic leverage on the nuclear program. As a revolutionary state, the Islamic Republic is willing to absorb a significant amount of pain and isolation in order to achieve "independence," regional power, and prestige. However, it will not be able indefinitely to stifle popular demands for a more democratic, accountable, and open political system. Consistent U.S. support for these values, espoused across the region and not just targeted at Iran, offers the best hope of eventually transcending the many differences that today separate the United States and Iran.

CHAPTER SIX

Policy Alternatives

Competing U.S. approaches toward Iran might be characterized as engagement versus containment, preemption versus deterrence, and normalization versus regime change. Each of these three theoretical alternatives offers a spectrum of choices to the policymaker.

A policy of pure engagement would emphasize the use of diplomacy to resolve differences while seeking to increase travel, cultural exchanges, and commerce between the United States and Iran. By contrast, a policy of pure containment would employ isolation, sanctions, and noncommunication to limit Iran's external influence and compel changes in its internal policies. Preemption goes beyond mere containment to include an offensive threat or use of military force to forestall some unwanted development—in Iran's case, the acquisition of a nuclear weapon capability. Deterrence, in contrast, would employ threats of retaliation to dissuade Iran from employing such weapons to influence, coerce, or damage others. Normalization would involve mutual diplomatic recognition, exchange of ambassadors, and reasonably civil discourse between the two governments, while regime change would involve the use of overt and covert efforts to delegitimize and destabilize the Iranian regime.

In effect, these are competing archetypes from which a more modulated policy can be constructed. Because much of the policy debate in the United States turns around these archetypes, it is useful to examine their characteristics and likely consequences if employed in isolation before turning to a synthesis that offers the best hope of advancing all three basic U.S. objectives: moderating Iran's external behavior, reforming its internal politics, and halting its nuclear program.

Engagement

The U.S. debate on engaging Iran usually revolves around the prospects for agreement, with the burden of proof resting with those advocating diplomacy to demonstrate that such an accord is indeed likely. As this monograph has suggested, the current leadership in Tehran shows little interest in a comprehensive settlement of its differences with Washington. Partial or tactical accommodations remain possible, but even these might be difficult to achieve. But such a standard for engagement misses an important point: Communication does not always produce agreement, but it almost invariably produces more information. Better information allows better policy.

During 40 years of cold war, communication between Washington and Moscow was constant, while agreements were few and far between. Even such agreements as were reached seldom touched the core issues dividing the two superpowers. Yet both sides adopted more-prudent policies as a result of these exchanges. Even when no agreements resulted, which was most of the time, both sides also influenced the policy of the other, and both sides benefited from having so done.

For more than 30 years, nearly as long as the Cold War with the Soviet Union, both Washington and Tehran have denied themselves these benefits. They have been content to make policy in the dark, more ignorant of the other side's intentions, anxieties, and policy deliberations than they needed to be. As a result, both sides have forgone many opportunities to influence the other, to avoid unnecessary confrontations, and to settle differences small and large.

Although it is true that engagement cannot guarantee accord, the absence of contact does guarantee disaccord. Hard-liners on both sides claim to oppose engagement because there is no possibility for mutual accommodation, but their real fear is just the opposite: that unfettered communication will eventually bring some rapprochement. The Iranian leadership fears that such rapprochement will tarnish its revolutionary credentials, while many U.S. opponents of engagement fear just the opposite: that any move to normalize relations with the Islamic Republic will enhance that regime's domestic and international legitimacy and, hence, its longevity. If history is any guide, the Iranian hard-liners have more reason to be concerned than the U.S. ones do. Regimes that the United States has engaged have been overthrown far more often than regimes that the United States has cold-shouldered. The Soviet Union, all of Eastern Europe, half a dozen countries in Latin America, the Philippines, Indonesia, and, most recently, Egypt and Tunisia are examples of the former, while Cuba, North Korea, and Iran are prime examples of the latter.

The absence of routinized communication has certainly led to missed opportunities to settle differences with Iran. The most recent occasion was in 2003, when the George W. Bush administration chose to ignore an attractive Iranian offer to negotiate out all outstanding differences because the U.S. administration doubted the offer's authenticity. The offer was real, if perhaps tentative, and could have been authenticated easily enough if the two capitals had been in regular and direct contact. The absence of communication has also occasioned unnecessary and tragic confrontations—for instance, when the U.S. Navy, in 1988, accidentally shot down an Iranian airliner full of innocent civilian passengers flying on a regular route in international airspace because it feared an Iranian attack

Containment

Since 1979, containment has been the dominant component of U.S. policy. As long as Iran remained surrounded by countries hostile to it, as was the case until 2001, this effort did not require major U.S. commitments. It was Iraqi, not Iranian, behavior, after all, that brought U.S. ground and air forces into the region in 1991 and has kept them there ever since. Containing Iran became much more difficult, however, once the United States had overthrown its two most-hostile neighbors. The new governments in Kabul and Baghdad are friendlier to the United States than their predecessors were, but they are also much friendlier toward Iran and much less capable of resisting Iranian influence.

The looming prospect of a nuclear-armed Iran will increase the costs of containment for the United States. Indeed, some analysts argue that it will be impossible to contain a nuclear-armed Iran, leaving the United States only the options of attack or retreat before Iran's burgeoning power.

Preemption

In his January 29, 2002, State of the Union address, President George W. Bush threatened military action against Iran, along with Iraq and North Korea, if these three regimes did not abandon their quests for nuclear weapons.[1] Washington has never explicitly withdrawn this threat, but Bush deemphasized it once the costs of occupying and rebuilding Iraq and Afghanistan, both much weaker and smaller countries than Iran, became apparent. Obama has been even more reticent on the topic.

An aerial attack, focused on Iran's known nuclear facilities, remains within the realm of domestic political feasibility for the United States. Much less costly than invasion and occupation, this option also offers much less assurance of ending the threat of an Iranian bomb. Then–Secretary of Defense Robert Gates indicated that such an attack could only slow, not halt, the Iranian program.[2] It is thought that the Iranians might already have secret facilities, ones about which the United States does not know and cannot bomb. In the wake of an attack, Iran would likely shift more of its nuclear program to such locations while redoubling resources committed to the effort.

Many argue that, even if the United States is unlikely to carry out a preemptive attack, it should continue to pose the threat for whatever effect this could have on Iranian calculations. This is a dubious proposition. Coercive diplomacy has a poor track record. Even very credible

---

[1]   Bush, 2002.

[2]   Klein, 2010.

threats often fail to secure the desired behavior change. As often as not, explicit threats only lead to more-obdurate behavior, making it necessary for the menacing state to either carry out its threat or ignominiously back down, with a consequent loss of credibility. This happened twice with Iraq under Saddam—once in 1990, when Saddam defied the U.S. ultimatum to evacuate Kuwait, and again in 2003, when he failed to document the dismantling of his WMD programs. Obduracy was also Serbia's President Milošević's reaction to NATO threats of an aerial attack in 1999 when he defied a NATO ultimatum to halt ethnic cleansing in Kosovo. In each of these cases, the threats had to be carried out before the desired result was achieved.

Threats, in the sense of fair warning as a prelude to war, serve a useful purpose in helping to establish the legitimacy of the subsequent attack. As a device to forestall conflict, however, they are less useful and can even be counterproductive, often making it more difficult for the adversary to change course without losing face. It would consequently be unwise for the United States to threaten an action that it had not already decided to carry out if necessary, and counterproductive to do so until all other paths had failed, because response to the threat would more likely be resistance to than adoption of the desired course of action.

Deterrence

It is sometimes suggested that containment is the alternative to preemption as Iran approaches the nuclear weapon threshold. This is wrong. The alternative to containment is invasion and occupation, not preemption. Containment has been U.S. policy since 1979. Containment would be the rationale for a preemptive strike designed to take out known Iranian nuclear facilities. Containment would remain U.S. policy in the aftermath of such an attack. The main argument against a preemptive strike is that it would actually make this subsequent containment more difficult. Iran would gain domestic support and international sympathy, particularly in the Muslim world.

Containment of a nuclear-armed Iran would differ from its present form in one important respect. It would need to include an element of nuclear deterrence, involving the extension of a U.S. nuclear umbrella over friends and allies in the region.

Normalization

In every capital around the world, the U.S. ambassador is a more important person than that country's ambassador in Washington. The U.S. ambassador has ready access to the local head of government, foreign and defense ministers, business leaders, press, and public. Most foreign ambassadors in Washington, even from the United States's most-powerful friends, seldom see U.S. cabinet officials, let alone the president, and their public pronouncements are seldom reported by the U.S. press. This is simply a reflection of the disparity in power between the United States and any other country.

In consequence of this disparity, the United States suffers more than Iran from the absence of diplomatic relations. A U.S. embassy in Tehran would be a far greater source of influence throughout that society than an Iranian mission in Washington would be. It would also be a far more valuable source of information for its home government. The United States is an open society whose policy debates can be followed from the media, whereas the workings of the Iranian regime are more opaque, putting a premium on in-place and confidential reporting. Tehran can learn far more from U.S. newspapers than Washington can from Iranian ones.

In fact, however, Iran already maintains a large official mission in New York and a smaller one in Washington (the latter is labeled the Iranian Interests Section of the Pakistan Embassy, but it is staffed by Iranian, not Pakistani officials). In contrast, there are no U.S. officials in Iran, nor do any visit there. Who, then, suffers most from this arrangement?

Regime Change

Although U.S. governments have been loath to admit it, Iran has, for much of the past 30 years, been more democratic than most U.S. allies in the region. This now is changing, as the balance of power within Iran shifts from pragmatists and reformers toward principlists and the Revolutionary Guards while significant parts of the Arab world might be moving in the other direction, toward more–genuinely representative government.

The Arab Spring has found inspiration in Western ideals, and some of its instigators received help and encouragement from publicly financed U.S. organizations, such as the National Endowment for Democracy and its Democratic and Republican affiliates. On the other hand, the decision by President Obama to cool the pro-democracy rhetoric of his predecessor was probably also helpful because it allowed indigenous Arab reformers to free themselves from any association with otherwise highly unpopular U.S. efforts at forced or coerced regime change.

The horrifically violent birth pangs of electoral politics in Iraq certainly gave pause to some would-be Iranian reformers. A failed transition to democracy in Egypt and Tunisia could produce a similar effect. On the other hand, if moderate, popularly based regimes in North Africa and even Syria do emerge, the example could encourage similar developments in Iran. Certainly, one of the lessons of democratization in Eastern Europe, Latin America, East Asia, and even parts of sub-Saharan Africa in the past 30 years has been the knock-on, contagious effects of such revolutions and the importance of peer pressure in bringing about such change. Working to promote successful transformations in several Arab countries is thus the best way the United States can work to encourage similar developments in Iran.

Conclusion

Clearly, no sensible U.S. policy can be based on the pure form of any of the alternatives described in this chapter. Pure engagement has little short- or even medium-term prospect of attaining any of the three main U.S. objectives. Containment affects only Iran's external behavior. Preemption deals only with the nuclear issue, and then only temporarily. Deterrence makes sense only if combined with containment and some minimal form of engagement, if only to prevent accidental disaster. Neither normalization nor regime change is a feasible short-term objective. Realistic policy must be fashioned at some intermediate point across each of these three spectrums.

CHAPTER SEVEN

Coping with a Nuclearizing Iran

It is not inevitable that Iran will acquire nuclear weapons, or even the capacity to quickly produce them. U.S. and even Israeli analysts continually push their estimates for such an event further into the future. Nevertheless, absent a change in Iranian policy, it is reasonable to assume that the day will come when Iran possesses such a capability. Western policymakers shy away from addressing this prospect, lest they seem to be acquiescing in something they deem unacceptable. But there is a big difference between acknowledging and accepting another's behavior. It is unacceptable that Iran should even be seeking nuclear weapons in violation of its treaty commitments, yet the U.S. government nevertheless acknowledges this behavior it cannot accept because that acknowledgment is a necessary prerequisite to effectively addressing the problem. By refusing to acknowledge the possibility of a nuclear weapon–capable Iran, the United States is inhibiting its capacity to deal successfully with the consequences of such a possible, indeed likely, development. Indeed, it is even inhibiting its ability to dissuade Iran from testing and deploying such weapons.

Theoretically, the spectrum of possible Iranian nuclear capability runs from no program, either civil or military, at one end, to a growing arsenal of tested weapons and long-range delivery systems at the other. Although the United States and much of the rest of the world would like to confine the Iranian program to the lowest possible level, there is very strong support within Iran, across its political spectrum, within and without the government, for full mastery of the nuclear fuel cycle. There even seems to be growing support within the general public in

Iran for acquiring nuclear weapons. RAND's 2009 survey of Iranian public opinion revealed that 43 percent of respondents favored the development of nuclear weapons. A subsequent survey by the International Peace Institute conducted in 2010 indicated even higher public support for nuclear weapons.[1] Given that the regime denies any intention of developing nuclear weapons and officially maintains that to do so would be un-Islamic, these figures are not the product of official propaganda. Rather, it appears that one unintended by-product of sanctions might be to increase Iranian popular sentiment in favor of acquiring nuclear weapons.

Nevertheless, sanctions remain an important element of containment, and containment of Iranian influence will be necessary as long as Iran employs subversion, terrorism, and ideology to destabilize its neighbors and threaten U.S. allies. However ineffective sanctions may be in altering the regime's intentions, they do affect its capabilities quite substantially. Sanctions degrade Iran's economy, its military capabilities, and its political stature, thereby limiting its ability to project power and influence. Sanctions retard Iran's nuclear program even if they increase domestic support for it. Sanctions will provide bargaining leverage if and when the Iranian regime changes for the better. Finally, penalizing Iranian violations of its NPT obligations is essential if other states are to be dissuaded from heading down a similar path.

The closer Iran moves toward testing and deploying nuclear weapons, the more negative the consequences for regional and global security. Uncertainty regarding Iran's actual capacity, although itself a source of anxiety, would be less provocative than certainty of such a capacity. The region has lived with an unacknowledged Israeli nuclear arsenal since the late 1960s and could conceivably do the same with a similarly discreet Iranian capacity. Better yet would be a certainty, derived from intrusive verification measures, that Iran, although capable of manufacturing nuclear weapons, had not actually done so. Worst of all would be a situation in which Iran had openly breached the NPT, tested and deployed nuclear weapons, and begun to articulate a doctrine for their use. This latter situation would be the most likely to prompt

---

[1]   Charney Research, 2010.

other states to go down this same path while maximizing the levels of tension and anxiety among regional governments and populations.

An objective of U.S. policy should be to roll back the Iranian nuclear program until that country is in full compliance with its NPT obligations. There is no step short of invading, overthrowing the regime, and occupying the country that could secure this goal in the short term. Therefore, without abandoning this longer-term goal, the more proximate U.S. objective should be to persuade Iran to halt its program short of building, testing, and deploying nuclear weapons. Doing so requires convincing the Iranian leadership that crossing this threshold will garner it more pain than gain.

Iran's leaders are seeking nuclear weapons for enhanced security, influence, and prestige. It is thus imperative to demonstrate to Iranian leaders that their country would become even more insecure, isolated, and penalized after it crossed the nuclear threshold than before. The best way to do so is to address the possibility, plan against it, and make clear to Iran how crossing a nuclear threshold will only solidify the rest of the world's determination to eventually see the process reversed. Talk of U.S. military preemption, which the Iranian regime does not believe, or of an Israeli strike, which it does not appear to fear, simply acts as a road block to the kind of international spadework needed to ensure that further advances in the Iranian program lead to increasingly severe penalties. Rather than closing off such international discussion, which is what threatening preemption does, the United States should be working to put in place arrangements that will further isolate and penalize Iran, contain its influence, discourage imitators, and build leverage against the day when a new leadership in Tehran can be persuaded to give up its nuclear armory.

Containment Plus

As noted, containment will remain at the core of U.S. policy as long as Iran continues to subvert and threaten its neighbors. This will be true whether or not Iran possesses a nuclear arsenal. It will be harder to achieve, however, if Iran crosses this threshold. It would be harder still to contain the influence of an Iran that had suffered an unprovoked U.S. or Israeli attack, an act that would provoke outrage and solidarity within Iran and sympathy abroad, particularly among (but not limited to) Muslim populations.

Containment of a nuclear-armed Iran will need to be complemented by deterrence, to counterbalance the threat of nuclear use or blackmail; by sanctions, to offer the eventual hope of rolling back that capability; by engagement, to manage such confrontations as might occur; and by the employment of soft power, in order to advance the day when containment will cease to be necessary. Only such a combination of policies offers the possibility of advancing all three main U.S. objectives.

Deterrence

The United States successfully deterred a much more powerful Soviet Union for more than 40 years, not just from attacking the United States, but from attacking any U.S. ally anywhere in the world. Some argue that Iran is different, that its leaders are irrational, and that the threat of devastating retaliation would not dissuade them from employing or threatening to employ nuclear weapons. Although this fear is understandable, given occasionally heated Iranian rhetoric, there is nothing in the Islamic Republic's actual behavior throughout its existence to substantiate the charge of irrationality, let alone suicidal lunacy. Compared with Joseph Stalin or Mao Zedong, Ayatollah Khamenei and President Ahmadinejad—whatever their other faults—are models of mental health and restrained behavior.

A more reasonable apprehension is not that nuclear deterrence would not work but rather that it would. A nuclear-armed Iran would be able to deter the United States from reacting forcefully to Iranian misbehavior. With the threat of U.S. (and Israeli) retaliation effectively removed, Iran could employ its nonmilitary instruments of influence even more aggressively than it has in the past.

This is certainly possible, but by no means inevitable. History does not suggest that states necessarily embark on riskier behavior once they acquire nuclear weapons. Soviet and Chinese policies actually moderated after they acquired nuclear weapons. A nuclear-armed Britain and France lost a string of colonial wars and abandoned their empires as a result. The one fairly clear-cut case of nuclear arms enabling risky behavior has been Pakistan's willingness to support high-profile terrorist attacks on India, which would almost certainly have occasioned Indian military retaliation had Pakistan not had a nuclear deterrent. So here again, deterrence worked, but not to India's advantage.

Given the Iranian regime's reliance on subversion and terrorism as instruments of influence, the acquisition of a nuclear shield might well increase Iranian risk-taking behavior. Historically, the mutual possession of nuclear weapons has always heightened the threshold of major conflict between adversaries and would almost certainly have the same effect were Iran to acquire such a capability. It is most unlikely that Iran would actually employ nuclear weapons for any reason short of regime preservation, particularly because it will remain inferior to all the other nuclear powers more or less indefinitely. So yes, the United States would have to forgo the option of invading a nuclear-armed Iran, overthrowing its regime, and occupying the country and would rather need to confine its response to any particular Iranian provocation short of outright aggression to something short of forced regime change. But the United States is already effectively deterred from such an option by the costs and consequences of such a step, without any need to worry about a nuclear response. Given crushing U.S. superiority across the entire military (and economic and political) spectrum, there are many potential responses available to the United States short of forced regime change with which to deter or punish Iranian transgressions. These will all remain available to the United States, and nuclear weapons would offer Iran no protection from such punitive steps.

Although Iran is most unlikely to employ nuclear weapons in circumstances short of defense of the regime, it might be tempted to adopt a more belligerent attitude in dealing with its neighbors and regional adversaries, particularly those without their own nuclear deterrent. The United States will thus have to stand ready to supply this counterweight, by extending its own nuclear umbrella over those friends and allies in the region that seek it.

The United States has already begun to put in place one element of such extended deterrence by arranging to provide Europe with a shield against Iranian missile attack. This investment would make little sense if the only threat were from conventionally armed Iranian missiles because the expense of the U.S.-proposed (and U.S.-financed) anti–ballistic missile (ABM) shield will far outweigh any damage Iran could do to Europe with high explosives. In beginning to deploy an ABM system in Europe, the United States has thus already begun to prepare for the "unacceptable": a nuclear-armed Iran.

The United States has also collaborated closely with Israel on ABM technology. As Iran moves toward a nuclear weapon capability, one will likely see similar U.S. support offered to other regional states.

Deploying defenses against Iranian nuclear attack involves what is called *deterrence by denial*—that is, physically denying the Iranians the capacity to conduct a successful attack. The United States is also likely to protect its friends and allies by extending the promise of *deterrence by punishment*—that is, retaliation. Given overwhelming U.S. military superiority, such a promise should represent a more credible form of deterrence than that which the United States extended over Cold War Europe. Then, the United States had to promise to commit suicide in defense of its European allies. Cold-war deterrence rested on what was accurately referred to as mutually assured destruction. In the case of Iran, U.S. guarantees will rely instead on the promise of unilaterally assured destruction because only one side (the United States) will possess the power to destroy the other.

Sanctions

Sanctions and other forms of persuasion should be deployed for both long- and short-term purposes. The long-term objective should be to bring Iran fully into compliance with the NPT. The short-term objective should be to halt the Iranian program short of weaponization. Achievement of both objectives will require the deft employment of carrots and sticks. Carrots should be deployed if Iran agrees to verification measures that convincingly demonstrate that it has not weaponized, but with enough sticks retained to provide a continuing incentive to eventually bring that country, perhaps under new leadership, back into full conformity with the NPT.

The current all-or-nothing U.S. approach, which insists on full rollback of enrichment as a prerequisite for any easing of sanctions, risks allowing the best to become the enemy of the good because neither the current nor any future regime in Iran is likely to agree to accept restrictions on its nuclear program beyond those required by the NPT. On the other hand, the full abandonment of sanctions in exchange for a promise not to weaponize, even if reliably monitored, would still leave Iran out of compliance with its other NPT obligations. Establishing and securing multilateral agreement to the right balance of carrots and sticks will be a tricky, but not impossible, diplomatic task. Getting the U.S. Congress to similarly agree to such a balanced approach might prove the higher hurdle.

Engagement

Diplomacy is unlikely to yield substantial breakthroughs as long as the current Iranian leadership remains in power. The United States nevertheless needs reliable channels of communication with the Iranian regime in order to garner information, signal warnings, avoid unintended conflict, and be positioned to move on openings toward accord when and if such arise. Should Iran actually build and deploy nuclear weapons, such channels of communication will become all the more important.

As noted earlier, President Obama has made several rather tentative efforts to open channels to the Iranian leadership. He spoke publicly to the Iranian people and sent two private messages to Khamenei, who is said to have responded tendentiously. In mid-2009, the U.S. State Department announced its intention to invite Iranian diplomats to U.S. embassies' Independence Day celebrations around the globe, only to withdraw the invitation a few days later, in deference to the Iranian demonstrators protesting President Ahmadinejad's allegedly fraudulent reelection.

Obama probably would have done better to address his private messages to President Ahmadinejad, who had earlier written both to him and before that to President George W. Bush and who seemed eager to garner the recognition that such a dialogue would provide him. Ahmadinejad now seems a spent force in Iranian politics, but, back in 2009, he had the backing of the Supreme Leader and considerable domestic popularity.

The State Department would also have been better off had it not tried to launch a working-level exchange with Iranian diplomats around the world in such a public, high-profile manner. It would have been more productive by far to have quietly lifted existing prohibitions on U.S. diplomats meeting with Iranians around the world in the normal course of their duties.

Interestingly, the George W. Bush administration, although much less committed to engagement in principle than its successor has been, did allow its ambassadors in Kabul and Baghdad to meet with their Iranian counterparts, and these conversations had some useful effect. It is hard to understand why Obama, having embraced the prospect of engagement with adversaries during the presidential campaign, should have barred his representatives from renewing such contacts. U.S. ambassadors in other capitals and at multinational posts, such as the UN and the IAEA, should be authorized to hold discussions with their Iranian counterparts within the framework of their existing responsibilities and instructions. These contacts should occur quietly and without fanfare. Eventually, if and when Tehran proves receptive, some privileged channel for more-comprehensive conversations could be established. The content and, indeed, the existence of these latter contacts should be closely held. This will be all the easier to do if the process of engagement is made a matter of routine.

Soft Power

Regime change is the best—maybe the only—path to better, more-cooperative relations between the United States and Iran. But explicit U.S. efforts to bring about that change, whether overt or covert, will probably have the reverse effect, helping perpetuate the current leadership. For the immediate future, therefore, the best thing Washington can do to encourage political reform in Iran is to help promote similar changes in other Middle Eastern countries where the United States has greater access and influence.

Adopting a region-wide and, indeed, globally consistent approach to democratization is important to establishing the credibility of U.S.

efforts. It is, of course, far easier to criticize one's enemies than one's friends, and more tempting to subvert one's adversaries than one's allies. Thus, for decades, the United States has vocally complained of lapses in Iranian democracy while working closely and uncritically with absolute monarchies that do not even hold elections or let the female half of their populations drive. President Bush's particularly strong emphasis on democratization, associated as it inevitably became with the troubled transformations of Iraq, Afghanistan, Lebanon, and the Palestinian territories, discomforted rather than encouraged regional reformers. Obama's more subdued approach to the topic has given these indigenous forces more space to identify democratic reform not with U.S. policy but with universal values and local aspirations.

Reformers in Iran are pressing for evolution, not revolution. The Green Movement is not seeking to overturn the Islamic Republic's unique mix of Islamic and democratic elements but rather to strengthen the latter. Oddly enough, President Ahmadinejad has been challenging the status quo from the other end of the political spectrum. In the short term, neither the Green Movement nor Ahmadinejad seems likely to succeed. But Iran has a young, reasonably well-educated population, one increasingly plugged into the world around it. Even as the United States seeks to isolate and penalize the Iranian regime for its external misbehavior and nuclear ambitions, it should be seeking to maximize the exposure of this population to the United States, to the West, and to the newly dynamic Middle East. By the same token, the United States should avoid association with separatist elements in Iran and extremist émigré groups that the vast bulk of the Iranian people reject.

Soft power is best envisaged more as a magnet than as a lever. The best way of employing the attractive elements of U.S. society is simply to remove barriers to exposure. Making Internet censorship more difficult is one means of so doing. Facilitating travel, commerce, and study abroad is also important. Sanctions erect barriers to this kind of exposure. This represents an unavoidable trade-off between the objectives of containment and the promotion of domestic reform, a trade-off that needs to be carefully weighed each time new sanctions are levied or old ones reconsidered.

Bibliography

al-'Abideen ar-Rukabi, Zain, "al-Natija: Kharab al-`Iraq wa Khidmat al-Iran wa Tadahur al-Iqtisad al-Amiriki" (The result: the destruction of Iraq, service to Iran, and the decline of the American economy), *al-Sharq al-Awsat Newspaper*, March 22, 2008.

Albright, Madeleine K., Secretary of State, "American-Iranian Relations," remarks before the American-Iranian Council, Washington, D.C., March 17, 2000.

Al-Dayni, Muhammad, "Kayfa Yandhuru al-Arab ila Iran?" (How do Arabs view Iran?), *al-Arabiya*, February 26, 2007.

Al-Humayd, Tariq, "American Withdrawal and the Second Stage," *Asharq Alawsat*, October 9, 2007.

————, "La Lil-Taslih al-'Iraq" (No to the arming of Iraq), *Asharq Alawsat*, September 10, 2008.

Allin, Dana H., and Steven Simon, *The Sixth Crisis: Iran, Israel, America and the Rumors of War*, New York: Oxford University Press, 2010.

"Al-Mashru' al-Irānī al-Iqlīmī wa al-Nawawī" (The Iranian regional and nuclear project), *Journal of King Khalid Military College*, January 6, 2009. As of August 16, 2011:
http://www.kkmaq.gov.sa/Detail.asp?InNewsItemID=319120

Al-Rintawi, Urayb, "Many Lessons," *Al-Dustour* (Jordan), June 10, 2010.

Alshayji, Abdullah K., "Mutual Realities, Perceptions, and Impediments Between the GCC States and Iran," in Lawrence G. Potter and Gary Sick, eds., *Security in the Persian Gulf: Origins, Obstacles, and the Search for Consensus*, New York: Palgrave, 2002, pp. 217–238.

"Azadi Qods Qafelgir Konand e Ast" (Jerusalem's liberation will be a surprise), *Jahan News*, February 2, 2011. As of October 14, 2011:
http://jahannews.com/vdcdxk0ffyt0kx6.2a2y.html

Baer, Robert, "Why Syria Will Keep Provoking Israel," *Time*, October 3, 2008. As of November 1, 2010:
http://www.time.com/time/world/article/0,8599,1846271,00.html

Bahgat, Gawdat, "Nuclear Proliferation: The Case of Saudi Arabia," *Middle East Journal*, Vol. 60, No. 3, Summer 2006, pp. 421–443.

Bahrampour, Tara, "Expats' 'Daily Show'–Style VOA Program Enthralls Iranians, Irks Their Government," *Washington Post*, December 31, 2010. As of August 15, 2011:
http://www.washingtonpost.com/wp-dyn/content/article/2010/12/31/AR2010123101327.html

Barzegar, Kayhan, "The Balance of Power in the Persian Gulf: An Iranian View," *Middle East Policy*, Vol. XVII, No. 3, Fall 2010, pp. 74–87.

Benn, Aluf, and Haaretz correspondent, "Obama's Atomic Umbrella: U.S. Nuclear Strike If Iran Nukes Israel," *Haaretz*, December 11, 2008. As of August 15, 2011:
http://www.haaretz.com/print-edition/news/obama-s-atomic-umbrella-u-s-nuclear-strike-if-iran-nukes-israel-1.259303

Black, Ian, "Arabs Ponder Implications of Iran's Unrest," *Guardian* (UK), June 25, 2009. As of August 15, 2011:
http://www.guardian.co.uk/world/2009/jun/25/ian-black-on-middle-east

Blanford, Nicholas, "Is Iran Driving New Saudi Diplomacy?" *Christian Science Monitor*, January 16, 2007. As of August 15, 2011:
http://www.csmonitor.com/2007/0116/p06s02-wome.html

Blechman, Barry M., Daniel Brumberg, and Steven Heydemann, *Engagement, Coercion, and Iran's Nuclear Challenge: Report of a Joint Study Group on US-Iran Policy*, Washington, D.C.: Stimson Center, 2010. As of October 14, 2011:
http://www.usip.org/files/resources/Engagement_Coercion_and_Irans_Nuclear_Challenge.pdf

Borger, Julian, "Iran Nuclear Talks in Istanbul: Is a Uranium Deal Back on the Table?" *Julian Borger's Global Security Blog (Guardian)*, January 20, 2011. As of October 14, 2011:
http://www.guardian.co.uk/world/julian-borger-global-security-blog/2011/jan/20/iran-nuclear-weapons

Bremmer, Ian, "Inside the Iranian Elite's Power Struggle," *Foreign Policy*, September 9, 2010. As of August 15, 2011:
http://eurasia.foreignpolicy.com/posts/2010/09/09/inside_the_iranian_elites_power_struggle_by_ian_bremmer

Broad, William J., John Markoff, and David E. Sanger, "Israeli Test on Worm Called Crucial in Iran Nuclear Delay," *New York Times*, January 15, 2011. As of October 14, 2011:
http://www.nytimes.com/2011/01/16/world/middleeast/16stuxnet.html

Brumberg, Daniel, and Barry Blechman, "Strategic Engagement with Iran," *Middle East Channel,* December 14, 2010. As of January 17, 2011:
http://mideast.foreignpolicy.com/posts/2010/12/14/
strategic_engagement_with_iran

Buchta, Wilfried, *Who Rules Iran? The Structure of Power in the Islamic Republic,* Washington, D.C.: Washington Institute for Near East Policy, 2000.

Bush, George W., "Address Before a Joint Session of the Congress on Administration Goals," February 27, 2001. As of August 18, 2011:
http://www.presidency.ucsb.edu/ws/index.php?pid=29643#axzz1VOkAjGCf

———, "Address Before a Joint Session of the Congress on the State of the Union," January 29, 2002. As of August 18, 2011:
http://www.presidency.ucsb.edu/ws/index.php?pid=29644#axzz1VOkAjGCf

Çağaptay, Soner, "Turkey's Transformation Under the AKP (III): Solidarity with Anti-Western and Islamist Regimes," *Hürriyet Daily News,* April 18, 2010. As of August 15, 2011:
http://www.hurriyetdailynews.com/n.php?n=turkey8217s-transformation-under-akp-iii-solidarity-with-anti-western-and-islamist-regimes-2010-04-18

Carden, Michael J., "Mullen: Diplomacy Best Approach to End Iran's Nuclear Proliferation," U.S. Department of Defense, April 18, 2010. As of August 15, 2011:
http://www.defense.gov/news/newsarticle.aspx?id=58792

Charney Research, "IPI Iran: National Survey," job 373, 702 telephone interviews with adult citizens of Iran, August 30–September 7, 2010. As of August 16, 2011:
http://www.ipacademy.org/images/pdfs/
cr_iran_2010_survey_frequency_questionnaire.pdf

Clapper, James R., director of national intelligence, Statement for the Record on the Worldwide Threat Assessment of the U.S. Intelligence Community for the House Permanent Select Committee on Intelligence, Washington, D.C., February 10, 2011. As of August 15, 2011:
http://www.dni.gov/testimonies/20110210_testimony_clapper.pdf

"Clinton, Qaboos to Work for Release of U.S. Hiker," Agence France-Presse, September 17, 2010.

"CNOOC Confirms Preliminary Gas Deal with Iran—Xinhua," Reuters, December 22, 2006. As of August 16, 2011:
http://uk.reuters.com/article/2006/12/22/
cnooc-iran-gas-idUKPEK17160720061222

Cohen, Roger, "The Making of an Iran Policy," *New York Times,* July 30, 2009. As of September 22, 2009:
http://www.nytimes.com/2009/08/02/magazine/02Iran-t.html

Cordesman, Anthony H., and Aram Nerguizian, "The Gulf Military Balance in 2010," Washington, D.C.: Center for Strategic and International Studies, April 23, 2010. As of June 6, 2010:
http://csis.org/publication/gulf-military-balance-2010-overview

D-8 Organization for Economic Cooperation, "Turkey, Iran Seeking to Boost Trade to $30 Billion," press release, Ankara, Turkey, February 6, 2010. As of October 14, 2011:
http://www.developing8.org/2010/02/06/
turkey-iran-seeking-to-boost-trade-to-30-billion/

Dalton, Richard, "Lessons from the EU-Iran Comprehensive Dialogue," in Patrick Clawson, ed., *Engaging Iran: Lessons from the Past*, Washington, D.C.: Washington Institute for Near East Policy, Policy Focus 93, May 2009, pp. 27–32. As of August 15, 2011:
http://www.washingtoninstitute.org/pubPDFs/PolicyFocus93.pdf

Daragahi, Borzou, "Iran's Revolutionary Guard Acknowledges Taking a Bigger Role in Nation's Security," *Los Angeles Times*, July 6, 2009.

———, "Iran Has Enough Fuel for 2 Nuclear Warheads, Report Says," *Los Angeles Times*, September 7, 2010. As of August 15, 2011:
http://articles.latimes.com/2010/sep/07/world/la-fg-iran-nuclear-report-20100907

Davis, Lynn E., Jeffrey Martini, Alireza Nader, Dalia Dassa Kaye, James T. Quinlivan, and Paul Steinberg, *Iran's Nuclear Future: Critical U.S. Policy Choices*, Santa Monica, Calif.: RAND Corporation, MG-1087-AF, 2011. As of August 15, 2011:
http://www.rand.org/pubs/monographs/MG1087.html

Dehghanpisheh, Babak, "Smugglers for the State: Sanctions Can't Touch the Revolutionary Guards' Black-Market Empire," *Newsweek*, July 10, 2010. As of August 15, 2011:
http://www.thedailybeast.com/newsweek/2010/07/10/smugglers-for-the-state.html

Director of National Intelligence, *Iran: Nuclear Intentions and Capabilities*, Washington, D.C., November 2007. As of August 16, 2011:
http://www.dni.gov/press_releases/20071203_release.pdf

Dobbins, James, "How to Talk to Iran," *Washington Post*, July 22, 2007. As of August 15, 2011:
http://www.washingtonpost.com/wp-dyn/content/article/2007/07/20/
AR2007072002056.html

———, *After the Taliban: Nation-Building in Afghanistan*, Washington, D.C.: Potomac Books, 2008.

———, "Our Man in Kabul: What Hamid Karzai's Rise to Power Means for How He Will Govern Now," *Foreign Affairs*, November 4, 2009. As of August 15, 2011:
http://www.foreignaffairs.com/articles/65669/james-dobbins/our-man-in-kabul

Düzel, Neşe, "İlter Türkmen: 'AKP'de İslam Romantizmi var'" (İlter Türkmen: "AKP has Islam romanticism"), *Taraf*, July 5, 2010. As of August 15, 2011:
http://www.taraf.com.tr/nese-duzel/
makale-ilter-turkmen-akp-de-islam-romantizmi-var.htm

Ehteshami, Anoushiravan, *After Khomeini: The Iranian Second Republic*, New York: Routledge, 1995.

El-Hokayem, Emile, and Matteo Legrenzi, "The Arab Gulf States in the Shadow of the Iranian Nuclear Challenge," Washington, D.C.: Stimson Center, May 26, 2006. As of August 16, 2011:
http://www.stimson.org/books-reports/
the-arab-gulf-states-in-the-shadow-of-the-iranian-nuclear-challenge/

Elson, Sara Beth, and Alireza Nader, *What Do Iranians Think? A Survey of Attitudes on the United States, the Nuclear Program, and the Economy*, Santa Monica, Calif.: RAND Corporation, TR-910-OSD, 2011. As of August 16, 2011:
http://www.rand.org/pubs/technical_reports/TR910.html

Erdbrink, Thomas, "Iran's Ahmadinejad Urges Backers to Eschew Violence in Campaign's Final Hours," *Washington Post*, June 11, 2009. As of August 15, 2011:
http://www.washingtonpost.com/wp-dyn/content/article/2009/06/10/
AR2009061003548.html

"Erdoğan: Kaynağımızı sanal düşmana harcadık" (Erdoğan: We spent our resources on a virtual enemy), *6News*, October 3, 2010. As of August 15, 2011:
http://www.6news.com.tr/tr/news/19592/
erdogan-kaynagimizi-sanal-dusmana-harcadik-

Esfandiari, Golnaz, "'Convincing' Revolutionary Guards Who Support Green Movement 'Better Than Eliminating Them,'" Radio Free Europe/Radio Liberty, July 26, 2010. As of August 15, 2011:
http://www.rferl.org/content/Convincing_Revolutionary_Guards_Support_
Green_Movement_Eliminating/2110049.html

Etzion, Eran, "The Ministry of Foreign Affairs Situation Assessment for 2008–2009," *Strategic Assessment*, Vol. 12, No. 1, June 2009, pp. 47–58. As of August 15, 2011:
http://www.inss.org.il/upload/(FILE)1244444840.pdf

Evron, Yair, "An Israel-Iran Balance of Nuclear Deterrence: Seeds of Instability," in Efraim Kam, ed., *Israel and a Nuclear Iran: Implications for Arms Control, Deterrence, and Defense*, Tel Aviv: Institute for National Security Studies, memorandum 94, July 2008, pp. 47–63. As of August 15, 2011:
http://www.inss.org.il/upload/(FILE)1216205527.pdf

Fairclough, Gordon, and Rebecca Blumenstein, "Turkey Questions Sanctions on Iran," *Wall Street Journal*, September 21, 2010, p. 11.

Fandy, Mamoun, "al-'Iraq: Ja'izat al-'Arab al-Kubra" (Iraq: the great Arab prize), *al-Sharq al-Awsat Newspaper,* June 9, 2008. As of August 15, 2011:
http://www.asharqalawsat.com/
leader.asp?section=3&issueno=10786&article=474218

Fassihi, Farnaz, "Iran's Economy Feels Sting of Sanctions," *Wall Street Journal,* October 12, 2010.

Freilich, Chuck, "The Armageddon Scenario: Israel and the Threat of Nuclear Terrorism," Begin-Sadat Center for Strategic Studies, Perspectives Papers on Current Affairs 104, April 8, 2010. As of August 15, 2011:
http://www.biu.ac.il/SOC/besa/perspectives104.html

Gasiorowski, Mark, "The New Aggressiveness in Iran's Foreign Policy," *Middle East Policy,* Vol. XIV, No. 2, Summer 2007, pp. 125–132.

Gause, F. Gregory III, "Saudi Arabia: Iraq, Iran, the Regional Power Balance, and the Sectarian Question," *Strategic Insights,* Vol. VI, No. 2, March 2007. As of August 15, 2011:
http://www.isn.ethz.ch/isn/Digital-Library/Publications/
Detail/?ots591=0c54e3b3-1e9c-be1e-2c24-a6a8c7060233&lng=en&id=30995

German Marshall Fund of the United States, *Transatlantic Trends: Key Findings 2010,* 2010. As of August 15, 2011:
http://trends.gmfus.org/?page_id=2729

Ghali, Ibrahim, "Russia wa al-Mihwar al-Mumana`in al-`Arab . . . Hudud al-`Alaqa" (Russia and the axis of Arab rejectionists: limits of the relationship) *IslamOnline,* October 28, 2007.

Guitta, Olivier, "First Target for Iran: Qatar?" *Middle East Times,* November 26, 2007.

Gundzik, Jephraim P., "The Ties That Bind China, Russia and Iran," *Asia Times,* June 4, 2005. As of August 15, 2011:
http://www.atimes.com/atimes/China/GF04Ad07.html

Guzansky, Yoel, "Compromising on a Nuclear Iran," *Strategic Assessment,* Vol. 12, No. 3, November 2009, pp. 87–96. As of August 15, 2011:
http://www.inss.org.il/upload/(FILE)1259658204.pdf

Hannah, John, "Is Saudi Arabia Ready to Play Hardball with Iran?" *Foreign Policy,* November 13, 2009. As of August 15, 2011:
http://shadow.foreignpolicy.com/posts/2009/11/13/
is_saudi_arabia_ready_to_play_hardball_with_iran

Hasan, Omar, "Kuwaiti MPs File Motion to Oust PM over Iran," *Iran Focus,* June 14, 2011.

Hashemi, Nader, and Danny Postel, *The People Reloaded: The Green Movement and the Struggle for Iran's Future,* Brooklyn, N.Y.: Melville House Publishing, 2010.

Henderson, Simon, "The Elephant in the Gulf: Arab States and Iran's Nuclear Program," Washington Institute for Near East Policy, PolicyWatch 1065, December 21, 2005. As of August 15, 2011:
http://www.washingtoninstitute.org/templateC05.php?CID=2424

Hirshman, Michael, "Gene Sharp: Theoretician of Velvet Revolution," Radio Free Europe/Radio Liberty, November 27, 2009. As of August 15, 2011:
http://www.rferl.org/content/Gene_Sharp_Theoretician_Of_Velvet_Revolution/1889473.html

İdiz, Semih, "HAMAS Türkiye'ye değil Mısır'a bakıyor" (Hamas looks up to Egypt, not to Turkey), *Milliyet*, June 14, 2010.

Ignatius, David, "Buying Time with Iran," *Washington Post*, January 9, 2011, p. 17. As of August 16, 2011:
http://www.washingtonpost.com/wp-dyn/content/article/2011/01/07/AR2011010703149.html

Inajima, Tsuyoshi, "Inpex Will Withdraw from Oil Project in Iran After Government Sanctions," *Bloomberg*, October 15, 2010. As of October 14, 2011:
http://www.bloomberg.com/news/2010-10-15/inpex-to-withdraw-from-azadegan-oil-project-in-iran-as-sanctions-increase.html

International Crisis Group, "U.S.-Iranian Engagement: The View from Tehran," Middle East Briefing 28, June 2, 2009. As of August 16, 2011:
http://www.crisisgroup.org/en/regions/middle-east-north-africa/iran-gulf/iran/B028-us-iranian-engagement-the-view-from-tehran.aspx

———, "Turkey and the Middle East: Ambitions and Constraints," Europe Report 203, April 7, 2010a. As of August 16, 2011:
http://www.crisisgroup.org/en/regions/europe/turkey-cyprus/turkey/203-turkey-and-the-middle-east-ambitions-and-constraints.aspx

———, "Turkey's Crises over Israel and Iran," Europe Report 208, September 8, 2010b. As of October 27, 2010:
http://www.crisisgroup.org/en/regions/europe/turkey-cyprus/turkey/208-turkeys-crises-over-israel-and-iran.aspx

"Iran to Give Hizbullah Weapons," *Jerusalem Post*, August 12, 2010. As of August 16, 2011:
http://www.jpost.com/MiddleEast/Article.aspx?id=184538

"Iran Hardliners Condemn Khatami," BBC News, May 6, 2008. As of October 18, 2010:
http://news.bbc.co.uk/2/hi/7386001.stm

Iran Human Rights Documentation Center, *Murder at Mykonos: Anatomy of a Political Assassination*, New Haven, Conn., 2007. As of August 16, 2011:
http://www.iranhrdc.org/english/publications/reports/3150-murder-at-mykonos-anatomy-of-a-political-assassination.html

"Iran Says Singapore Frees 3 Impounded Iranian Ships," *Voice of America News*, January 5, 2011. As of October 14, 2011:
http://www.voanews.com/english/news/middle-east/
Iran-Says-Singapore-Frees-3-Impounded-Iranian-Ships-112945199.html

"Iran Tuhadid Duwal al-Khalij al-Muta'awinah ma' America bil Sawarikh" (Iran threatens the Gulf countries cooperating with America with missiles), *Al-Sharq al-Awsat Newspaper*, July 11, 2007.

"Israel Wants More Stealth Fighters," *DefenseNews*, December 15, 2010. As of October 14, 2011:
http://www.defensenews.com/story.php?i=5243057

"Israelis Ponder the Perils of Hitting Iran," UPI, December 30, 2009. As of August 16, 2011:
http://www.upi.com/Top_News/Special/2009/12/30/
Israelis-ponder-the-perils-of-hitting-Iran/UPI-45971262208365/

"İsrail yeni hava sahası bakıyor" (Israel is looking for a new airspace), *ntvmsnbc*, April 16, 2010. As of August 16, 2011:
http://www.ntvmsnbc.com/id/25082638

Issacharoff, Avi, "Turkish Forces Foil Hezbollah Attack on Israeli Target," *Haaretz*, September 12, 2009. As of August 16, 2011:
http://www.haaretz.com/print-edition/news/
turkish-forces-foil-hezbollah-attack-on-israeli-target-1.2529

Kaplan, Seth, "A New U.S. Policy for Syria: Fostering Political Change in a Divided State," *Middle East Policy*, Vol. XV, No. 3, Fall 2008. As of August 16, 2011:
http://www.mepc.org/journal/middle-east-policy-archives/
new-us-policy-syria-fostering-political-change-divided-state

Katz, Mark, "Russian-Iranian Relations in the Ahmadinejad Era," *Middle East Journal*, Vol. 62, No. 2, Spring 2008.

———, "Russia Balks at New Pressure on Iran," *Iran Primer*, March 16, 2011. As of April 27, 2011:
http://iranprimer.usip.org/blog/2011/mar/16/russia-balks-new-pressure-iran

Katz, Yaakov, "Security and Defense: Israel Goes Ballistic," *Jerusalem Post*, September 10, 2009a, p. 15. As of August 16, 2011:
http://www.jpost.com/Features/FrontLines/Article.aspx?id=154524

———, "Israel, US to Simulate Response to Regional War During Missile Defense Drill," *Jerusalem Post*, October 11, 2009b, p. 2.

———, "Juniper Cobra Exercise Here to Help US Design European Missile Shield," *Jerusalem Post*, November 1, 2009c, p. 2.

Kaye, Dalia Dassa, and Frederic M. Wehrey, "A Nuclear Iran: The Reactions of Neighbours," *Survival*, Vol. 49, No. 2, Summer 2007, pp. 111–128.

Kechichian, Joseph A., *Oman and the World: The Emergence of an Independent Foreign Policy*, Santa Monica, Calif.: RAND Corporation, MR-680-RC, 1995. As of August 16, 2011:
http://www.rand.org/pubs/monograph_reports/MR680.html

Keinon, Herb, "Amid Shifting Regional Sands, Mullen Reaffirms US-Israeli Strategic Ties," *Jerusalem Post*, February 15, 2011, p. 2.

Kerr, Paul, "Iran Agrees to Temporarily Suspend Uranium-Enrichment Program," *Arms Control Today*, December 2004. As of August 16, 2011:
http://www.armscontrol.org/act/2004_12/Iran

Kessler, Glenn, "In 2003, U.S. Spurned Iran's Offer of Dialogue," *Washington Post*, June 18, 2006. As of August 16, 2011:
http://www.washingtonpost.com/wp-dyn/content/article/2006/06/17/AR2006061700727.html

———, "U.S. Withdraws July 4th Invite to Iranian Diplomats," *Washington Post*, June 24, 2009. As of October 14, 2011:
http://voices.washingtonpost.com/44/2009/06/24/us_withdraws_july_4th_invite_t.html?wprss=44

Khalaji, Mehdi, *The Last Marja: Sistani and the End of Traditional Religious Authority in Shiism*, Washington, D.C.: Washington Institute for Near East Policy, Policy Focus 59, September 2006. As of August 16, 2011:
http://www.washingtoninstitute.org/templateC04.php?CID=250

———, "The Problems of Engaging with Iran's Supreme Leader," Washington, D.C.: Washington Institute for Near East Policy, PolicyWatch 1426, November 12, 2008. As of August 16, 2011:
http://washingtoninstitute.org/templateC05.php?CID=2960

Khalaji, Mehdi, and Patrick Clawson, "Quds Day in Iran: Velvet Revolution Trumps Nuclear Negotiations," Washington, D.C.: Washington Institute for Near East Policy, PolicyWatch 1580, September 17, 2009.

"Kırmızı Kitap'ta Köklü Değişim" (Fundamental change in Red Book), *Milliyet*, June 28, 2010.

Klein, Joe, "An Attack on Iran: Back on the Table," *Time*, July 15, 2010. As of October 14, 2011:
http://www.time.com/time/magazine/article/0,9171,2004120,00.html

Kralev, Nicholas, and Barbara Slavin, "Ex–Defense Chief Met with Tehran Aide," *Washington Times*, January 30, 2009. As of September 22, 2009:
http://www.washingtontimes.com/news/2009/jan/30/ex-defense-secretary-meets-with-tehran-aide/

120 Coping with a Nuclearizing Iran

Kramer, Heinz, *AKP's "New" Foreign Policy Between Vision and Pragmatism*, Berlin: Stiftung Wissenschaft und Politik, Deutsches Institut für Internationale Politik und Sicherheit, working paper FG 2 2010/01, June 2010. As of August 16, 2011:
http://www.swp-berlin.org/fileadmin/contents/products/arbeitspapiere/Krm_WP_Neu_ks.pdf

"Kuwaiti MPs File Motion to Oust PM Over Iran," Agence France-Presse, June 14, 2011.

Lawson, Fred H., "Syria's Relations with Iran: Managing the Dilemmas of Alliance," *Middle East Journal*, Vol. 61, No. 1, Winter 2007, pp. 29–47.

Leverett, Flynt, "Iran: The Gulf Between Us," *New York Times*, January 24, 2006. As of August 16, 2011:
http://www.nytimes.com/2006/01/24/opinion/24leverett.html

Leverett, Flynt Lawrence, and Jeffrey Bader, "Managing China-U.S. Energy Competition in the Middle East," *Washington Quarterly*, Vol. 29, No. 1, Winter 2005–2006, pp. 187–201. As of August 16, 2011:
http://muse.jhu.edu/journals/wq/summary/v029/29.1leverett.html

Leverett, Flynt L., and Hilary Mann Leverett, "The United States, Iran and the Middle East's New 'Cold War,'" *International Spectator*, Vol. 45, No. 1, 2010, pp. 75–87.

Levitt, Matthew, "Financial Sanctions," *Iran Primer*, 2010. As of August 16, 2011:
http://iranprimer.usip.org/resource/financial-sanctions

Limbert, John W., *Negotiating with the Islamic Republic of Iran*, Washington, D.C.: U.S. Institute of Peace, Special Report 199, January 2008. As of August 16, 2011:
http://www.usip.org/publications/negotiating-islamic-republic-iran

Lindsay, James M., and Ray Takeyh, "After Iran Gets the Bomb: Containment and Its Complications," *Foreign Affairs*, March–April 2010.

MacFarquhar, Neil, "U.N. Approves New Sanctions to Deter Iran," *New York Times*, June 9, 2010. As of October 14, 2011:
http://www.nytimes.com/2010/06/10/world/middleeast/10sanctions.html

Majidyar, Ahmad, "Russo-Iranian Relations from Iran's Perspective," *Iran Tracker*, American Enterprise Institute, May 20, 2009. As of August 16, 2011:
http://www.irantracker.org/analysis/russo-iranian-relations-irans-perspective

Melman, Yossi, "Ex–Mossad Chief Dagan: Military Strike Against Iran Would Be 'Stupid,'" *Haaretz*, May 8, 2011. As of August 15, 2011:
http://www.haaretz.com/print-edition/news/ex-mossad-chief-dagan-military-strike-against-iran-would-be-stupid-1.360412

Middle East Media Research Institute, "Recent Saudi-Iranian Contacts to Resolve the Lebanon Crisis," Special Dispatch Series, January 26, 2007.

Milani, Abbas, "Iran: A Coup in Three Steps," *Forbes*, June 15, 2009. As of August 16, 2011:
http://www.forbes.com/2009/06/15/
iran-elections-khamenei-mousavi-ahmadinejad-opinions-contributors-milani.html

Miller, Greg, and Joby Warrick, "U.S. Report Finds Debate in Iran on Building Nuclear Bomb," *Washington Post*, February 18, 2011. As of August 16, 2011:
http://www.washingtonpost.com/wp-dyn/content/article/2011/02/18/
AR2011021805632.html

Mohammadi, Majid, "Green Movement: Islamist or Secularist," *Gozaar*, April 26, 2010. As of August 16, 2011:
http://www.gozaar.org/english/articles-en/
Green-Movement-Islamist-or-Secularist.html

"Moqtada al Sadr: Dar Sourat e Fesharhay e Tehran, Iran Ra Tark Mikonam" (Moqtada al Sadr: I'll leave Iran in the face of pressures from Tehran), *Jarash News*, November 20, 2010. As of August 16, 2011:
http://www.rahesabz.net/story/14262/

Moubayed, Sami, "'President' Larijani: A Star Is Born," *Asia Times*, June 21, 2008. As of August 16, 2011:
http://www.atimes.com/atimes/Middle_East/JF21Ak02.html

"MPs, Media Hype Hiking Sectarian Tension Locally," *Arab Times*, March 27, 2011. As of August 26, 2011:
http://www.arabtimesonline.com/NewsDetails/tabid/96/smid/414/ArticleID/
167260/reftab/96/Default.aspx

Nader, Alireza, and Joya Laha, *Iran's Balancing Act in Afghanistan*, Santa Monica, Calif.: RAND Corporation, OP-322-MCIA, 2011. As of August 16, 2011:
http://www.rand.org/pubs/occasional_papers/OP322.html

Nahmias, Roee, "Turkish Official Says Iran Sanctions Will Hurt Region," *Ynetnews*, June 9, 2010. As of August 16, 2011:
http://www.ynetnews.com/articles/0,7340,L-3902668,00.html

Naïm, Mouna, "Riyadh Solicits Damascus to Alleviate Lebanese Tensions," *Le Monde*, January 26, 2007, p. 4.

Nasseri, Ladane, "Ahmadinejad Has Harmed Iran's Dignity, Mousavi Says (Update2)," *Bloomberg*, June 4, 2009. As of October 16, 2010:
http://www.bloomberg.com/apps/news?pid=newsarchive&sid=aqFkjAOCEdw4

Nye, Joseph S. Jr., "Soft Power and American Foreign Policy," *Political Science Quarterly*, Vol. 119, No. 2, Summer 2004, pp. 255–270.

Obaid, Nawaf, "Stepping into Iraq," *Washington Post*, November 29, 2006. As of August 16, 2011:
http://www.washingtonpost.com/wp-dyn/content/article/2006/11/28/
AR2006112801277.html

Özel, Soli, "İran ve seçimler" (Iran and elections), *Habertürk*, June 13, 2010. As of August 16, 2011:
http://www.haberturk.com/yazarlar/523198-iran-ve-secimler

Parsi, Trita. *Treacherous Alliance: The Secret Dealings of Israel, Iran, and the United States*, New Haven, Conn.: Yale University Press, 2007.

Partrick, Neil, "Dire Straits for US Mid-East Policy: The Gulf Arab States and US-Iran Relations," Royal United Services Institute, January 9, 2008. As of August 16, 2011:
http://www.rusi.org/analysis/commentary/ref:C4784DF6A9E6B2/

Posch, Walter, "Iran and the European Union," *Iran Primer*, U.S. Institute of Peace, 2010. As of August 16, 2011:
http://iranprimer.usip.org/resource/iran-and-european-union

Prusher, Ilene R., "To Defend Against Iran Missiles, US and Israel Conduct Joint Exercises," *Christian Science Monitor*, October 29, 2009. As of August 16, 2011:
http://www.csmonitor.com/World/Middle-East/2009/1029/p06s33-wome.html

Public Law 104-172, Iran and Libya Sanctions Act of 1996, August 5, 1996. As of August 16, 2011:
http://www.gpo.gov/fdsys/pkg/PLAW-104publ172/html/PLAW-104publ172.htm

Public Law 109-293, Iran Freedom Support Act, September 30, 2006. As of August 16, 2011:
http://frwebgate.access.gpo.gov/cgi-bin/
getdoc.cgi?dbname=109_statutes2_at_large&docid=2p120stats-5

Public Law 111-195, Comprehensive Iran Sanctions, Accountability, and Divestment Act of 2010, July 1, 2010. As of August 16, 2011:
http://www.gpo.gov/fdsys/pkg/PLAW-111publ195/html/PLAW-111publ195.htm

Putrich, Gayle S., "U.S. Deploys Radar, Troops to Israel," *Defense News*, September 26, 2008. As of August 16, 2011:
http://www.defensenews.com/story.php?i=3744319

Qadura, Kamal, "'Opek lil-Ghaz' . . . Hulm am Haqiqa?" (An OPEC for gas: dream or reality?), *al-Sharq al-Awsat Newspaper*, May 2, 2008.

Rogers, Paul, *Military Action Against Iran: Impact and Effects*, Oxford Research Group Briefing Paper, July 2010. As of August 16, 2011:
http://www.oxfordresearchgroup.org.uk/publications/briefing_papers/
military_action_against_iran_impact_and_effects

Rozen, Laura, "Revealed: Recent U.S.-Iran Nuclear Talks Involved Key Officials (Updated)," *Foreign Policy*, January 30, 2009. As of September 22, 2009:
http://thecable.foreignpolicy.com/posts/2009/01/29/
americas_secret_back_channel_diplomacy_with_iran

Saab, Bilal Y., "Syria and Iran Revive an Old Ghost with Defense Pact," Brookings, July 4, 2006. As of November 1, 2010:
http://www.brookings.edu/opinions/2006/0704MiddleEast_Saab.aspx

Sadjadpour, Karim, *Reading Khamenei: The World View of Iran's Most Powerful Leader*, Carnegie Endowment for International Peace, March 2008a. As of August 16, 2011:
http://www.carnegieendowment.org/2008/03/10/
reading-khamenei-world-view-of-iran-s-most-powerful-leader/3dt

———, "U.S. Engagement with Iran: A How to Guide," *Middle East Bulletin*, Carnegie Endowment for International Peace, November 25, 2008b. As of August 16, 2011:
http://carnegieendowment.org/2008/11/25/
u.s.-engagement-with-iran-how-to-guide/1p90

———, "Iran: Recent Developments and Implications for U.S. Policy," testimony before the U.S. House of Representatives Committee on Foreign Affairs, July 22, 2009. As of September 22, 2009:
http://www.carnegieeurope.eu/publications/?fa=23419

Sadr, Ehsaneh I., "The Impact of Iran's Nuclearization on Israel," *Middle East Policy*, Vol. XII, No. 2, Summer 2005, pp. 58–72.

Sadr, Shahryar, "How Hezbollah Founder Fell Foul of Iranian Regime," *Mianeh*, July 12, 2010.

Schmidt, Michael S., "Iraq Cracks Down on Iran-Backed Shiite Militias," *New York Times*, July 1, 2011. As of August 16, 2011:
http://www.nytimes.com/2011/07/02/world/middleeast/02iraq.html

Shaffer, Brenda, *Partners in Need: The Strategic Relationship of Russia and Iran*, Washington, D.C.: Washington Institute for Near East Policy, 2001.

Shanahan, Rodger, *The Gulf States and Iran: Robust Competitors or Interested Bystanders?* Sydney: Lowy Institute for International Policy, November 2009. As of August 16, 2011:
http://www.lowyinstitute.org/Publication.asp?pid=1160

Sharma, Rakesh, "India, Iran to Continue Oil Payment Talks," *Wall Street Journal*, May 31, 2011.

Shenna, John C., "The Case Against the Case Against Iran: Regionalism as the West's Last Frontier," *Middle East Journal*, Vol. 64, No. 3, Summer 2010, pp. 341–363. As of August 16, 2011:
http://muse.jhu.edu/journals/the_middle_east_journal/v064/64.3.shenna.html

Siamdoust, Nahid, "Protestors Cry, 'It's Not Possible,'" *Time*, June 13, 2009. As of August 16, 2011:
http://www.time.com/time/world/article/0,8599,1904563,00.html

Simon, Steven, "An Israeli Strike on Iran," Council on Foreign Relations, CPA Contingency Planning Memorandum 5, November 2009. As of August 26, 2011:
http://www.cfr.org/israel/israeli-strike-iran/p20637

Singh, Michael, "Changing Iranian Behavior: Lessons from the Bush Years," in Patrick Clawson, ed., *Engaging Iran: Lessons from the Past*, Washington, D.C.: Washington Institute for Near East Policy, Policy Focus 93, May 2009, pp. 24–26. As of August 16, 2011:
http://www.washingtoninstitute.org/pubPDFs/PolicyFocus93.pdf

Slavin, Barbara, *Mullahs, Money, and Militias: How Iran Exerts Its Influence in the Middle East*, Washington, D.C.: U.S. Institute for Peace, June 2008. As of August 16, 2011:
http://www.usip.org/publications/
mullahs-money-and-militias-how-iran-exerts-its-influence-middle-east

Solomon, Jay, "Senior Democrat Snubbed by Iran in Outreach Bid," *Wall Street Journal*, February 2, 2009. As of August 16, 2011:
http://online.wsj.com/article/SB123352824260337327.html

———, "Bahrain Sees Hezbollah Plot in Protest," *Wall Street Journal*, April 25, 2011. As of August 16, 2011:
http://online.wsj.com/article/
SB10001424052748703907004576279121469543918.html

Solomon, Jay, and Charles Levinson, "Sanctions Slow Iran's Warhead Capability," *Wall Street Journal*, January 8, 2011, p. 1. As of August 16, 2011:
http://online.wsj.com/article/
SB10001424052748704739504576067911497955494.html

Stack, Megan K., "Hands-Off or Not? Saudis Wring Theirs Over Iraq," *Los Angeles Times*, May 24, 2006. As of August 16, 2011:
http://articles.latimes.com/2006/may/24/world/fg-saudi24

Stewart, Phil, "Gates, in Riyadh, Seeks Saudi Help on Iran Sanctions," Reuters, March 10, 2010a. As of August 16, 2011:
http://www.reuters.com/article/2010/03/10/
us-usa-saudi-gates-idUSTRE62957V20100310

———, "Gates Sees Iran Rift, Says Strike Would Unite Country," Reuters, November 16, 2010b. As of August 16, 2011:
http://www.reuters.com/article/2010/11/16/
us-usa-iran-gates-idUSTRE6AF3G720101116

Stracke, Nicole, "GCC and the Challenge of US-Iran Negotiations," Gulf Research Center, March 5, 2009. As of August 16, 2011:
http://grc.kcorp.net/?frm_action=view_newsletter_web&sec_
code=grcanalysis&frm_module=contents&show_web_list_link=1&int_content_
id=60339

Swartz, Spencer, and Benoît Faucon, "Iran's Falling Oil Output Means Less Revenue, Clout," *Wall Street Journal*, June 26, 2010. As of August 16, 2011:
http://online.wsj.com/article/
SB10001424052748704569204575328851816763476.html

Takeyh, Ray, *Hidden Iran: Paradox and Power in the Islamic Republic*, New York: Times Books, 2006.

―――, "Shaping a Nuclear Iran: The West's Diplomatic Goal Needs to Move from 'Suspension' to 'Transparency,'" *Washington Post*, May 18, 2008, p. B7.

Taşpınar, Ömer, "The Anatomy of Turkey's Iran Policy (I)," *Today's Zaman*, July 26, 2010a. As of August 16, 2011:
http://www.todayszaman.com/tz-web/
columnists-217169-the-anatomy-of-turkeys-iran-policy-i.html

―――, "The Anatomy of Turkey's Iran Policy (II)," *Today's Zaman*, August 2, 2010b. As of October 21, 2010:
http://www.todayszaman.com/tz-web/
columnists-217860-the-anatomy-of-turkeys-iran-policy-ii.html

Thaler, David E., Alireza Nader, Shahram Chubin, Jerrold D. Green, Charlotte Lynch, and Frederic Wehrey, *Mullahs, Guards, and Bonyads: An Exploration of Iranian Leadership Dynamics*, Santa Monica, Calif.: RAND Corporation, MG-878-OSD, 2010. As of August 16, 2011:
http://www.rand.org/pubs/monographs/MG878.html

Toukan, Abdullah, and Anthony H. Cordesman, *Study on a Possible Israeli Strike on Iran's Nuclear Development Facilities*, Washington, D.C.: Center for Strategic and International Studies, March 14, 2009. As of August 16, 2011:
http://csis.org/files/media/csis/pubs/090316_israelistrikeiran.pdf

Treaty on the Non-Proliferation of Nuclear Weapons, July 1, 1968.

"Trilateral Talks Rattle Gulf States While Concealing Complex Iranian Dynamics," *Gulf States Newsletter*, Vol. 31, No. 807, June 8, 2007.

"Turkish Foreign Ministry Denies Hezbollah Arms Claims as Baseless," *Hürriyet Daily News*, August 13, 2010. As of August 16, 2011:
http://www.hurriyetdailynews.com/
n.php?n=turkish-foreign-ministry-denies-hezbollah-claims-as-baseless--2010-08-13

"Turkish Foreign Policy: The Great Mediator—Sometimes Turkey Really Is a Bridge Between West and East," *Economist*, August 19, 2010. As of August 15, 2011:
http://www.economist.com/node/16847136

"Turkish President Voices Concern over Military Action on Iran," *Hürriyet Daily News*, September 22, 2010. As of August 15, 2011:
http://www.hurriyetdailynews.com/
n.php?n=gul-voices-concern-over-military-action-on-iran-2010-09-22

"Türkiye artık çantada keklik değil" (Turkey is no more piece of cake), *T24*, September 25, 2010. As of August 16, 2011:
http://www.t24.com.tr/haberdetay/100737.aspx

UNHCR—*See* United Nations High Commissioner for Refugees.

United Nations High Commissioner for Refugees, "Statistics on Displaced Iraqis Around the World," September 2007. As of August 16, 2011:
http://www.unhcr.org/470387fc2.html

———, "Iraqi Refugees in Syria Reluctant to Return to Home Permanently: Survey," Geneva, October 8, 2010. As of August 16, 2011:
http://www.unhcr.org/4caf376c6.html

United Nations Security Council, "Security Council Imposes Sanctions on Iran for Failure to Halt Uranium Enrichment, Unanimously Adopting Resolution 1737 (2006)," Department of Public Information, News and Media Division, New York, SC/8928, December 23, 2006a. As of August 16, 2011:
http://www.un.org/News/Press/docs/2006/sc8928.doc.htm

———, resolution 1737 (2006), S/RES/1737 (2006), December 27, 2006b.

———, resolution 1747 (2007), S/RES/1747 (2007), March 24, 2007a.

———, "Security Council Toughens Sanctions Against Iran, Adds Arms Embargo, With Unanimous Adoption of Resolution 1747 (2007)," Department of Public Information, News and Media Division, New York, SC/8980, March 24, 2007b. As of August 16, 2011:
http://www.un.org/News/Press/docs/2007/sc8980.doc.htm

———, resolution 1803 (2008), S/RES/1803 (2008), March 3, 2008a.

———, "Security Council Tightens Restrictions on Iran's Proliferation-Sensitive Nuclear Activities, Increases Vigilance Over Iranian Banks, Has States Inspect Cargo," Department of Public Information, News and Media Division, New York, SC/9268, March 3, 2008b. As of August 16, 2011:
http://www.un.org/News/Press/docs/2008/sc9268.doc.htm

———, resolution 1929 (2010), S/RES/1929 (2010), June 9, 2010.

U.S. Energy Information Administration, "China," Country Analysis Brief, last updated July 14, 2010a. As of August 16, 2011:
http://www.eia.gov/countries/country-data.cfm?fips=CH

———, "Iran," Country Analysis Brief, last updated July 14, 2010b. As of August 16, 2011:
http://www.eia.gov/countries/country-data.cfm?fips=IR

———, "Russia," Country Analysis Brief, last updated July 14, 2010c. As of August 16, 2011:
http://www.eia.gov/countries/country-data.cfm?fips=RS

"U.S. Not in a Position to Attack Iran: IRGC Commander," *Tehran Times*, August 12, 2010. As of August 16, 2011:
http://old.tehrantimes.com/index_View.asp?code=224688

Warrick, Joby, "Iran's Natanz Nuclear Facility Recovered Quickly from Stuxnet Cyberattack," *Washington Post*, February 16, 2011. As of August 16, 2011:
http://www.washingtonpost.com/wp-dyn/content/article/2011/02/15/
AR2011021505395.html

Wehrey, Frederic, Jerrold D. Green, Brian Nichiporuk, Alireza Nader, Lydia Hansell, Rasool Nafisi, and S. R. Bohandy, *The Rise of the Pasdaran: Assessing the Domestic Roles of Iran's Islamic Revolutionary Guards Corps*, Santa Monica, Calif.: RAND Corporation, MG-821-OSD, 2009. As of August 16, 2011:
http://www.rand.org/pubs/monographs/MG821.html

Wehrey, Frederic M., and Dalia Dassa Kaye, "Fifth Columns in the Gulf?" *Foreign Policy*, May 24, 2010. As of August 16, 2011:
http://mideast.foreignpolicy.com/posts/2010/05/24/fifth_columns_in_the_gulf

Wehrey, Frederic, Dalia Dassa Kaye, Jessica Watkins, Jeffrey Martini, and Robert A. Guffey, *The Iraq Effect: The Middle East After the Iraq War*, Santa Monica, Calif.: RAND Corporation, MG-892-AF, 2010. As of August 16, 2011:
http://www.rand.org/pubs/monographs/MG892.html

Wehrey, Frederic, David E. Thaler, Nora Bensahel, Kim Cragin, Jerrold D. Green, Dalia Dassa Kaye, Nadia Oweidat, and Jennifer J. Li, *Dangerous but Not Omnipotent: Exploring the Reach and Limitations of Iranian Power in the Middle East*, Santa Monica, Calif.: RAND Corporation, MG-781-AF, 2009. As of August 15, 2011:
http://www.rand.org/pubs/monographs/MG781.html

Worth, Robert F., "Iran's Leader Cements Ties on State Visit to Lebanon," *New York Times*, October 13, 2010a. As of August 16, 2011:
http://www.nytimes.com/2010/10/14/world/middleeast/14lebanon.html

———, "Iran's President Praises Hezbollah," *New York Times*, October 14, 2010b. As of October 20, 2010:
http://www.nytimes.com/2010/10/15/world/middleeast/15lebanon.html

Worth, Robert F., Heather Timmons, and Landon Thomas Jr., "Crisis Puts Focus on Dubai's Complex Relationship with Abu Dhabi," *New York Times*, November 29, 2009. As of August 16, 2011:
http://www.nytimes.com/2009/11/30/business/global/30dubai.html

Wright, Robin B., ed., *The Iran Primer: Power, Politics, and U.S. Policy*, Washington, D.C.: U.S. Institute of Peace, 2010.

Yaari, Ehud, "Iran's Nuclear Program: Deciphering Israel's Signals," Washington, D.C.: Washington Institute for Near East Policy, PolicyWatch 1597, November 5, 2009. As of August 16, 2011:
http://www.washingtoninstitute.org/templateC05.php?CID=3135

Yacoubian, Mona, "Syria's Alliance with Iran," U.S. Institute of Peace, Peace Brief, May 2007. As of August 16, 2011:
http://www.usip.org/publications/syria-s-alliance-iran

Yetkin, Murat, "Davutoğlu: Bugün İran'a, yarın Türkiye'ye" ("Davutoğlu: today against Iran, tomorrow against Turkey), *Radikal*, September 25, 2010.

Zacharia, Janine, "Adviser to Israel's Netanyahu Questions Mideast Peace Effort, New Iran Sanctions," *Washington Post*, June 23, 2010, p. 6. As of August 16, 2011:
http://www.washingtonpost.com/wp-dyn/content/article/2010/06/22/AR2010062204690.html

Zand-Bon, "250 Members of the Revolutionary Guard Supporters of Mousavi, Being Forced to Retire," *Planet Iran*, July 30, 2010. As of August 16, 2011:
http://planet-iran.com/index.php/news/20043

Zeynalov, Mahir, "Tehran, Ankara Vie to Gain Influence over Gaza," *Today's Zaman*, June 18, 2010. As of August 16, 2011:
http://www.todayszaman.com/tz-web/news-213449-tehran-ankara-vie-to-gain-influence-over-gaza.html